THE BROOKLYN PHILHARMONIC ORCHESTRA
salutes the sponsors of its 1993/94 SOUNDWAVE season and donors to

The Russian Stravinsky

Leadership support for THE RUSSIAN STRAVINSKY has been provided by

The Division of Public Programs, Public Humanities Projects
of the National Endowment for the Humanities,
Selectimpex Bank of Moscow, Russia
and the
Trust for Mutual Understanding.

The 1993/94 SOUNDWAVE Season is sponsored by Philip Morris Companies Inc.

BPO's Russian Stravinsky Gala, celebrating the Orchestra's 40th Anniversary, has been made possible
by Republic National Bank of New York and Republic Bank for Savings.

BPO is proud to be the recipient of a National Endowment for the Arts Challenge III Grant.

A program companion, edited by Joseph Horowitz,
for a weekend festival exploring the folk roots of early Stravinsky.

Presented by the Brooklyn Philharmonic Orchestra
at the Brooklyn Academy of Music, May 6, 7, and 8, 1994

Editorial Assistant/Production Manager: Lisa B. Segal
Illustrations Consultant: Anna Tavis
Book Design: Caren Hector/Chip Blazer

The Russian Stravinsky

May 6, 7, and 8, 1994

The Brooklyn Philharmonic Orchestra at The Brooklyn Academy of Music

Our Stravinsky weekend poses formidable assignments

for everyone involved. The conductors and musicians have prepared some of the most challenging works in Western music, and it is with an unusually high level of excitement, anticipation, and even tension that we arrive at the moment of performance.

Igor Stravinsky has in great part defined what the twentieth century symphony orchestra is about. At the same time, his marvelous and exultant creations have flung down a gauntlet for modern music. From The Rite of Spring *to* Requiem Canticles, *this is a great and important achievement. Deal with it!*

I hope that after this weekend we will have all gained insight into the creative process and the motives of a sublime artist. We will certainly be helped in identifying the Russian spirit which is actually waiting to be discovered in practically everything Stravinsky wrote. But beyond the musical and aesthetic questions certain to be considered looms a larger, potentially explosive field of discussion to which issues of nationalism and politics will inevitably lead. Perhaps learning how great artists of the past dealt with the terrifying political, moral, and economic chaos around them can be useful to us today; the parallels to our own times are chilling. At the very least we can learn to admire artists for their art, athletes for their skill and courage, politicians for their tact and ingenuity, without transferring to them the responsibility for our own moral inadequacies.

Dennis Russell Davies
Principal Conductor
Brooklyn Philharmonic Orchestra

4

Ivan Bilibin, Illustration of the Firebird, 1899

Table of Contents

Why the Russian Stravinsky?

INTRODUCTION
by Joseph Horowitz

A quarter century after his death, Igor Stravinsky more than ever looms as the twentieth century's most famous composer of "serious" music. But Stravinsky's geographical and stylistic odysseys make him hard to place. Born in Russia in 1882, he lived abroad beginning in 1910. He spent World War I in Switzerland. He moved to Paris in 1920. He became a French citizen in 1934. He settled in Hollywood from 1940 to 1969. He became an American citizen in 1945. He died in New York in 1971. He is buried in the Russian corner of a Venetian cemetery.

The dominant Western tendency has been to regard Stravinsky as an international modernist. Spurning Romanticism and its national schools, he reinvigorated more chaste aesthetics in pursuit of an art-for-art's sake ideal of pure, depersonalized beauty. "Music," he once wrote, "is given to us to establish an order in things; to order the chaotic and the personal into something perfectly controlled, conscious and capable of lasting vitality." Transcending politics and race, his idiom — according to conventional wisdom — is essentially cosmopolitan, with strong roots in the French avant-garde. In fact, Stravinsky sometimes called himself "French." *In Chroniques de ma vie* (1936), he proclaimed France his "second motherland." A 1937 Chicago headline reported: "Stravinsky, in German, Says He's French."

Pierre Boulez, in an influential 1953 analysis, exhaustively diagrammed the organization of "rhythmic themes" in *The Rite of Spring* (or *Le sacre du printemps,* or *Vesna svyashchennaya*) and discovered intimations of serialism. This compositional method, beginning in Vienna and Berlin with Schoenberg's 12-tone rows and proceeding in gathering waves of density to Boulez himself, carried modernist complexity to an hermetic extreme. And it is true that Stravinsky himself, after World War II, became an exceptionally communicative serialist composer — an astonishing accommodation to Germanic music the Francophile Stravinsky had disdained.

One of the most eagerly awaited musicological studies in recent years is Richard Taruskin's forthcoming *Stravinsky and the Russian Traditions,* scheduled for publication next year. The central proposition of this two-volume tome — a book as vigorous as it is massive — is that Stravinsky is not ultimately French, or German, or cosmopolitan. Rather, he is "the most completely 'Russian' composer of art music that ever was, and, if present trends continue, that ever will be." In Taruskin's account, Stravinsky achieved artistic maturity by absorbing the traditions of Russian folk music. And he was crucially influenced, in this absorption, not only by his Russian upbringing, but also by Sergei Diaghilev's *Mir iskusstva* ("World of Art") circle — by the world of Diaghilev's Ballet Russes, and its "Silver Age" writ-

ers and painters. And yet, Taruskin continues, *Mir iskusstva's* emphasis on folklore eventually embarrassed Stravinsky — he associated it with Red Russia, where an art "national in form and socialist in content" had become a cultural norm.

* * *

At the heart of Taruskin's project is a detailed examination of Stravinsky's relationship to rural song and ritual, including texts and melodies collected by the folklorists Fyodor Istomin, Yevgeniya Linyova, and Piotr Vasilyevich Kireyevsky — collections Stravinsky knew and utilized. As it happens, while Taruskin was writing his book, a present-day Russian folklorist was conducting field work with the same objective: uncovering Stravinsky's kinship to mother Russia. And, like Taruskin, Dmitri Pokrovsky concluded that Stravinsky's intimacy with Russian oral traditions had been underestimated — and not least by Stravinsky himself.

Pokrovsky began his research while a music student in the early 1970s. As he later recalled: "One day, as I wandered around northern Russia, I walked up a village road. In the distance I heard the voices of women, singing. As I got closer, I saw five very old women singing *loudly* — more loudly than a modern rock group. Their voices, in unison, had incredible resonance. Those voices touched feelings deep inside me, feelings that are hard to define. It was a moment of great discovery. I felt that I had been lost and now I was found. I had found the music of ancient Russia. And so my quest began."

Pokrovsky's quest took him to villages in southern and western Russia where Stravinsky had travelled around the turn of the century. He tape-recorded and transcribed the old songs. Rural Russia's links to its archaic, pre-Christian past, he discovered, had not completely disappeared. And neither had the links to early Stravinsky. In *Chroniques de ma vie,* the émigré composer had written of his *Les noces:*

> I borrow[ed] nothing from folk pieces, with the exception of the theme of one factory song in the last tableau, which I repeat several times on different texts. All the other themes, motives and melodies are of my

own composition . . . The recreation of a country wedding ritual . . . which in any case, I never had the chance either to see or listen to . . . absolutely didn't enter my mind. Ethnographic questions occupied me very little.

But the wedding music Pokrovsky heard in western Russia and the Ukraine corresponded — in structure, in method, in countless obscure details — to the marriage rites of *Les noces.*

Igor Stravinsky

9

As an aspect of his research, Pokrovsky in 1973 created the Dmitri Pokrovsky Ensemble, whose members accompanied him in the field. The ensemble, Pokrovsky included, learned the exotic wails and ululations that Pokrovsky the ethnomusicologist documented. Having amassed a repertoire of more than 2,000 songs, the ensemble now turns to the music of Stravinsky himself. Its new recording of *Les noces,* on Elektra/Nonesuch, is unlike any previous Stravinsky performance. Negating the more tempered dynamics and cooler timbres of schooled concert singers, applying the vocal techniques of the peasants Stravinsky allegedly heard (and allegedly forgot), it aspires to return this music to the village earth from which it issued. At BAM, the Pokrovsky Ensemble performs *Les noces* (for the first time in New York) and *Renard* (for the first time anywhere), as well as source materials — ceremonies, dances, songs — for both these works and for *The Rite of Spring.*

* * *

A further dimension of the Russian Stravinsky, as explored this weekend, is supplied by Russian visual art. In the West, the relationship of Stravinsky to Russian dance is well appreciated — as is Russian dance itself. But the Ballet Russes was only one part of Diaghilev's "World of Art." Emulating Wagnerian *Gesamtkunstwerk, Mir iskusstva* equally embraced poetry, scenic design, and painting. Nicolas Roerich, Natalia Goncharova, Mikhail Larionov — names insufficiently known to Americans — were eminent Stravinsky collaborators whose paintings and designs infused the style and content of his music.

In *Stravinsky and the Russian Traditions,* Taruskin cites the work of John E. Bowlt and Elizabeth Kridl Valkenier, distinguished art historians who participate in our BPO weekend. Bowlt writes of *Mir isskustva:*

> The graphic expertise in the decorative pieces of these artists might be seen, in broader terms, as the result of their non-philosophical approach to art; because without definite ideological justification their art was left to turn in on itself, to manipulate to the fullest estent its own properties of line, color, mass.

The same strengths and weaknesses, Taruskin argues, apply to Stravinsky's *Fireworks* (1909), in which line, color, and mass substitute for previous preoccupations with harmony and thematic form.

Taruskin's exhaustive correlation of turn-of-the-century Russian music with turn-of-the-century Russian visual art may be summarized as follows:

— Beginning in the 1860s, the powerful critic Vladimir Stasov championed parallel movements in Russian music and art. In music, the "Mighty Five" — Balakirev, Borodin, Cui, Mussorgsky, and Rimsky-Korsakov — rejected European Classicism in favor of folkloric topics and materials. In art, the *Peredvizhniki* (or "Wanderers") — including Ilya Repin, the most famous Russian painter of the late nineteenth century — similarly repudiated academicism for specifically Russian and rural themes.

— Late, decadent phases of both these movements paradoxically embraced the very academicism they originally spurned. In a "precise analogy," both currents veered away from nationalism; even Rimsky claimed: "Russian music does not exist." And such early Stravinsky as the Symphony in E-flat, *Scherzo fantastique,* and *Fireworks* is less explicitly "Russian" than his *Firebird* and *Petrushka* to come. Out of this cloistered aesthetic environment certain young talents, Stravinsky included, freed themselves by means of *Mir iskusstva.*

— In a crucial transformation, the avant-garde turned neo-nationalist. In visual art, the combination of Western *art nouveau* with Russian crafts and antiquities resulted in a Russian *jugendstil,* a movement including Mikhail Vrubel and Roerich. This was *Mir iskusstva* in its ripest phase. Its most famous single product was Stravinsky's *The Rite of Spring,* with scenario and design by Roerich.

— Probing its own archaic, pre-Christian roots, neo-nationalism evolved into a neo-primitivism whose principal practitioners included Goncharova and Larionov — collaborators with Stravinsky on *Les noces* and *Renard,* respectively.

— Ultimately, *Mir isskustva* is not a "radical" movement comparable to Scriabin's mystical

piano sonatas or Alexander Blok's fin-de-siécle symbolist poetry. Notwithstanding its early propagation of modernism, it remained essentially conservative. The *Mir isskustva* artists and musicians were formalists, concerned not with feelings or "higher" themes, but with craftsmanship and style.

* * *

Richard Taruskin and Dmitri Pokrovsky meet for the first time this weekend at BAM. Judging from the evidence of the present booklet (the "Interview with Dmitri Pokrovsky," for instance), the resulting dialogue will disclose broad areas of agreement about the Russian Stravinsky — and also areas of disagreement over the precise nature of Stravinsky's debt to oral tradition. The participation of John E. Bowlt and Elizabeth Kridl Valkenier will enlarge the dialogue to include such figures as Repin, Roerich, Goncharova, and Larionov. And, prodded by Taruskin (as in the notes on *The Rite of Spring, Renard*, and *Les noces* that follow), we broach one final dimension of the Russian Stravinsky: politics.

Taruskin is a tireless crusader against a view with which Stravinsky was prominently identified: that art represents itself and nothing more. Composers, writers, painters, Taruskin believes, are not as morally indifferent as we may think. In the twentieth century, he continues, we have withdrawn our attention from the political messages of art — even when those messages are inhumane, and are conveyed by the most conspicuous and influential practitioners. Among European modernist composers, he finds Bartók, an outspoken anti-fascist, the exception, not the rule. In fascist Italy, modernism was fashionable; even Luigi Dallapiccola, who was the leading Italian serialist composer, and whose wife was Jewish, at one time followed the Duce. In Austria, Webern admired the Nazis. Even Schoenberg, who eventually returned to Judaism, praised his own 12-tone method for insuring "the supremacy of German music . . . for the next hundred years." As for Stravinsky — this member of the untitled nobility, disinherited from considerable property by the Soviets, was, Taruskin tells us, contemptuous of liberalism and democracy prior to his migration to America, and prone to anti-Semitism to the end of his life.

In an article in *The New Republic* (September 5, 1988), Taruskin quotes a letter Stravinsky wrote to his publisher shortly after Hitler took power: "I am surprised to have received no proposals from Germany for next season, since my negative attitude toward communism and Judaism — not to put it in stronger terms — is a matter of common knowledge." Stravinsky recorded his *Jeu de cartes* with the Berlin Philharmonic in 1938. "His only response to the Nazi persecutions," Taruskin adds, "was to ask (in another letter to his publisher): 'Is it politically wise vis-a-vis Germany to identify myself with Jews like Klemperer and Walter, who are being exiled?'" Stravinsky's longtime friend and amanuensis Robert Craft responded at length to Taruskin in *The New York Review of Books* (February 16, 1989). Stravinsky's anti-Semitism, while not excusable, must be understood in context, Craft argued. "Anti-Semitic remarks between White Russians, like anti-*goy* remarks between Jews, are not invariably, or even usually — so one must believe — expressions of deep hatreds." Stravinsky, Craft added, performed in public (as opposed to his 1938 studio recording) only once in Nazi Germany — "against his will and under pressure from his German publisher."

These issues are discomfiting. Are they relevant to the Russian Stravinsky? Readers of this book, audiences at these concerts, will judge for themselves.

The Russian Stravinsky

Stravinsky and Russia: Why the Memory Hole?

by Richard Taruskin

If Stravinsky will be remembered as the most famous twentieth century composer, he is not necessarily the best known or understood. The story of his life—and, even more so, of his musical development—teems with riddles. The biggest of them concern his musical origins and his early ("Russian") period, despite the fact that it was the period of his most famous works, and despite the voluminous Stravinsky literature, so much of it contributed by the composer himself. For as his career proceeded along its spectacular course he became increasingly embarrassed by his past and did all he could to force it down an Orwellian memory hole. He did this not only by withholding or suppressing information, but also, more subtly, by supplying it in selective superabundance. His various accounts of his early years, given at various points during his later ones, all contradict one another, and all are in greater or lesser conflict with the ascertainable facts.

Whence this celebrated mendacity? It stemmed, one has to conclude, not just from a faulty memory or from indifference to factual accuracy, but from an astonishing, chronic sense of cultural inferiority that reached a besetting climax near the end of Stravinsky's career, leaving him doubtful about the validity of his work and fretful about his place in history. Robert Craft informs us that "all of his life...Stravinsky complained that he had been handicapped in his

youth by his isolation from an intellectually stimulating environment." Compensation is everywhere apparent in Stravinsky's writings, with their obsessively recherché vocabulary and self-conscious (and, given the author, notably gratuitous) insistence on his "advanced" technique. But its most stunning manifestation was something no one could have expected before the period of the serial music and the "conversations" books with Craft: his acknowledgment of the reality and the legitimacy of the Germanic "mainstream" that he had devoted a career (and for many, very persuasively) to denying. Once Stravinsky had crossed this bridge, his whole past became useless to him. Earlier he had assumed with special vehemence and authority the archly ironic tone Russian composers had habitually adopted when speaking of German music. In interviews of the twenties, Stravinsky spoke of the "nefarious influence in Russia of German music," and claimed that "each time that the influence of French and Italian music has been felt in Russia, the result has been an opening up, a flowering." By the thirties, newly a citizen of France, he proudly identified himself with French culture, both in word and in musical deed.

But sour grapes were ever fermenting behind this façade; for, like all Russian composers, Stravinsky envied the Germans their traditions. The mask fell when it became so terribly impor-

tant for him to establish belated and retroactive connections with the New Vienna School. Typical of Stravinsky the serialist were self-pitying assertions like this one, from *Dialogues and a Diary:* "I am a double émigré, born to a minor musical tradition and twice transplanted to other minor ones." What astonishes here is the assessment of French music, which he went on to describe as being, at the time of his "removal" to it, "almost as eclectic as 'Russian music,' and even less 'traditional.'"

Comparison of the seven cursory pages allotted to "St. Petersburg" in the 1959 *Conversations with Igor Stravinsky* (roughly equal to the space devoted to "Schoenberg, Berg, Webern") with the account of his early years in *Chroniques de ma vie* will suffice to show how squeamish Stravinsky had become about his Russian apprenticeship. In the *Chroniques* he had been quite candid, if apologetic, about his early acceptance of the academic views of the so-called Belyayev circle, and in particular, about his early admiration for Glazunov.

> I was then of an age—the age of early apprenticeship—when the critical faculty is generally lacking, and one blindly accepts truths propounded by those whose prestige is unanimously recognized, especially where this prestige is concerned with the mastery of technique and the art of *savoir faire.* Thus I accepted their dogmas quite spontaneously, and all the more readily because at the time I was a fervent admirer of Rimsky-Korsakov and Glazunov. I was specially drawn to the former by his melodic and harmonic inspiration, which then seemed to me full of freshness; to the latter by his feeling for symphonic form; and to both by their scholarly workmanship.

One gets the impression that Stravinsky had bent over backward to praise his colleague Glazunov—possibly because Glazunov was still alive and residing, like Stravinsky, in Paris.

In *Conversations,* Stravinsky bent over just as far in the opposite direction:

> The first concert of which I have any recollection was the occasion of a *première* of a

symphony by Glazunov. I was nine or ten years old and at this time Glazunov was the heralded new composer. He *was* gifted with extraordinary powers of ear and memory, but it was going too far to assume from that that he must be a new Mozart; the sixteen-year-old prodigy was already a cut and dried academician. I was not inspired by this concert.

The most patent fib in *Conversations* concerns the one early Stravinsky piece that rates an extended discussion in the book. Craft asked whether Stravinsky had had Maeterlinck's *La vie des abeilles* in mind as a program for his *Scherzo fantastique* of 1908. Here is Stravinsky's reply:

> No, I wrote the Scherzo as a piece of "pure" symphonic music. The bees were a choreographer's idea....I have always been fascinated by bees,...but I have never attempted to evoke them in my work (as, indeed, what pupil of the composer of the *Flight of the Bumble Bee* would?)...

And here is an extract from a letter Stravinsky sent Rimsky-Korsakov from Ustilug on 18 June 1907 (O.S.), published in the Soviet Union two years after Stravinsky's death:

> I am working a great deal. This work consists of orchestrating the Symphony and composing a fantastic Scherzo, "The Bees," about which I'll tell you more....As you know, I already had the idea of writing a scherzo in St. Petersburg, but as yet I had no subject for it. Then all at once here Katya [Stravinsky's wife] and I were reading "The Life of the Bees" by M. Maeterlinck, a halfphilosophical, half-poetical work that captivated me, as the saying goes, from head to toe. At first I thought, for the sake of the fullness of the program, that I would choose some specific citations from the book, but I see now that that is impossible, since the scientific and literary language is too closely intermixed in it, and therefore I decided that I would simply allow myself to be guided in composing the piece by a definite program, but not use any citation as a heading. Simply "The Bees" (after Maeterlinck): Fantastic Scherzo.

There can hardly be any question of a lapse of memory in a matter so fundamental. Stravinsky intended, quite simply, to deceive. But the deception was anything but cynical. Indeed, it was principled: Stravinsky badly needed to dissociate himself from an artistic milieu that put such stock in program music that one could not so much as begin writing a scherzo without having some definite "subject" in mind.

"Pure music," in any case, was always a sensitive point for the Parisian and American Stravinsky. "Folklore" was another—the touchiest of all, in fact, for its associations with the Red Russia Stravinsky abhorred, where an art "national in form and socialist in content" (in Stalin's words) had become a watchword. In *Conversations,* Stravinsky kept totally silent on the matter of folklore in his own work, even when his Diaghilev scores were touched upon in a section entitled the "Painters of the Russian Ballet."

The one overt reference to folklore in *Conversations* came in a startling paragraph on Bartók, where Stravinsky let it be known that "I could never share his lifelong gusto for his native folklore. This devotion was certainly real and touching, but I couldn't help regretting it in the great musician." Let us only recall that in the period of his first fame, from *Firebird* to *Les noces,* Stravinsky was universally cited as the single Russian composer of his generation to carry forward the Russian nationalism of his forebears. However much it may prove necessary to qualify that evaluation when it comes to individual works, the basic truth of it lies too close to the surface to require documentary confirmation as such.

Another side of Stravinsky's deep-seated ambivalence about his past came unexpectedly (but in retrospect, of course, inevitably) to the fore during his brief eightieth-birthday-year visit to his native country in the fall of 1962. At the "deeply Dostoevskian dinner" tendered him at Moscow's Metropole Hotel by the Soviet Ministry of Culture on the evening of 1 October—an occasion unforgettably described by Robert Craft—Stravinsky blurted out with quasi-involuntary suddenness to the assembled company, including Shostakovich, Khachaturyan, and

Khrennikov, that "a man has one birthplace, one fatherland, one country—he *can* have only one country—and the place of his birth is the most important factor in his life." Four days earlier, in an interview published in *Komsomolskaya pravda,* he had confided that "I have spoken Russian all my life, I think in Russian, my way of expressing myself [*slog*] is Russian. Perhaps this is not immediately apparent in my music, but it is latent there, a part of its hidden nature."

Since Stravinsky's death the uncovering of this immanent Russianness has become a major focus of research. This has been particularly true in the Soviet Union, where a number of valuable studies of Stravinsky's music, seen as it were from the inside, and some even more valuable documentary publications have appeared in the course of the last couple of decades. Though the prime source of documentation for Stravinsky's early period is gone forever owing to military and political vicissitudes, much can still be done to firm up a picture of Stravinsky's musical development by examining the early works against the background of the music that surrounded them. But to accomplish this it is necessary first to set the historical scene with the aid of a broad range of documentary material relevant to the period of Stravinsky's development: the St. Petersburg musical press, the arts journals of the period, and particularly the work of art historians whose approach to what is often called the "Silver Age" of Russian culture has never been emulated up to now by historians of music.

With regard to the masterpieces of Stravinsky's early maturity, a question that has especially interested the Soviet Stravinsky scholars who have emerged in the period since his death: that of "folklore and modernity," as the composer Sergei Slonimsky has phrased it. For what is remarkable about the period that begins with *Firebird* is the fecundating influence of folklore, approached in a manner unprecedented in the work not just of Stravinsky, but of any previous Russian composer. As a young Soviet musicologist has observed, "Exceptional mastery allowed Stravinsky to maintain a specifically national quality in practically all the works of the Russian period....The striving for national character distinguishes Stravinsky from many foreign com-

Stravinsky at the age of 15.

out, along with the irony implicit in the fact that Stravinsky achieved his greatest national character precisely at the point where he passed beyond the time-honored method of securing it—that is, by the actual quotation of folk music.

Most attempts at dealing with these questions have been hampered by some groundless but durable assumptions. The common conception in the West of a Russian composer—and by now, to be sure, in Russia as well—is one of a musician who imbibes folklore with his mother's milk. And most writers on Stravinsky have risen to the bait their subject scattered tendentiously in the *Chroniques* and in the conversations (the peasant with the musical armpit; the Yarmolintsy fair; the St. Petersburg knife grinder) and portrayed him as a natural folklorist. But Stravinsky came of age in a musical milieu that upheld a banner of "denationalization" in Russian music and scorned "gusto for native folklore" almost as much as Stravinsky would do in his remarks about Bartók.

Stravinsky was *converted* to folklore as a musical resource by the same new friends who had rescued him from academicism—that is, the painters and esthetes of Diaghilev's *Mir iskusstva* ("World of Art") circle—and these two facets of their influence on him were profoundly symbiotic. To find the sources of Stravinsky's folklorism, then, one must go outside the history of Russian music altogether and look to the history of Russian painting and theatrical design.

The period following *The Rite of Spring* and particularly following the outbreak of World War I, when Stravinsky became an exile from Russia no longer by choice but by force of circumstances, coincided with a preoccupation with folklore unparalleled in the history of Russian music—one that so conditioned every aspect of his work along essentially non-European lines that the word "Eurasian" comes to mind.

Eurasianists saw Russia as a thing apart from Europe (and from Asia as well), a separate land-

posers of the same period, and played no small role in his quest for renewed musical resources."

But not even this formulation goes far enough toward defining Stravinsky's somewhat paradoxical and ambiguous relationship to the folk traditions of his native land. The Russian word *zarubezhnïy,* normally translated as "foreign" (as in the quote above), literally means "beyond the frontiers." But that, ironically enough, was where Stravinsky was located at the time of his greatest striving for national character. And while such strivings did indeed set him off from such "foreign" contemporaries as Strauss, Schoenberg, and (maybe) Debussy (though not, obviously, from Bartók), they set him no less apart from his modernist contemporaries back home. Where is the national character in Scriabin? In Myaskovsky? Even in the young Prokofiev? These ironies need to be addressed and sorted

17

Nikolai Rimsky-Korsakov, to whom Stravinsky was closely attached from the age of 20.

mass (they called it "Turanian"), a separate world. In its most radical manifestations Eurasianism was wholly a product (like Stravinsky's "Swiss" music) of the postrevolutionary emigration. Thus, the Swiss years were conditioned by an idea of Russia and of Russian culture that did not and could not exist inside Russia. One of Stravinsky's more perceptive early Soviet critics caught this irony well when he wrote, "In approaching closer than any Russian composer to the presentation of the real Russian folk-life, Stravinsky did so just when that life was already becoming a legend, irretrievable, and incapable of regeneration in its original living form." It was the special mission of the Eurasianists to cling fast to that legend, to (as Nicolas Nabokov once put it about *Les noces*) "retrieve the irretrievable by re-inventing it." For them it was—it had to be—reality.

Even as he cultivated the façade of a sophisticated cosmopolitan, then, Stravinsky was profoundly un- and even anti-Western in his musical thinking (and much more so than any previous Russian composer had cause to be). Inevitably, the Eurasian aspects of the style worked out in his "period of exploration and discovery" marked him for life. They remained with him as permanent stylistic resources, however neoclassic or neoserial his overt stylistic orientation would become. He was, ultimately, an outsider to all traditions of West and East alike—at first a triumphantly self- proclaimed outsider, at last a humbled and suppliant outsider, but at all times the great *"zarubezhnïy"* of twentieth-century music.

The sources that must illuminate this phase of Stravinsky's development include the documents surrounding the World of Art movement and the journal *Mir iskusstva* itself; the work of the new breed of Russian ethnographers and musical folklorists of Stravinsky's generation; the annals of the Ballets Russes; and a broad spectrum of cultural materials relevant to the Russian "Silver Age" (poetry and belles lettres, art and art criticism). This means culling the work of anthropologists, historians, philosophers, poets, dramatists, and literary critics in search of anything that might have a bearing on the backgrounds to the masterworks of the Russian years. Where appropriate, one may also consult the writings of musicians.

In summation, one may put the newly emergent view of "Stravinsky and the traditions" in the form of five propositions:

1) That Stravinsky achieved artistic maturity and his modernist technique by deliberately playing the traditions of Russian folk music against those of the provincial, denationalized Russian art music in which he had been reared.

2) That he came to his knowledge of folklore, and his attitudes concerning its creative utilization, not from his musical training, but from his association with the artists of the "World of Art" circle.

3) That he deliberately retained that which was most characteristically and exclusively Russian in his musical training and combined it with stylistic elements abstracted from Russian folklore in a conscious effort to excrete from his style all that was "European."

4) That the stylistic synthesis thus achieved formed him as a composer for life, whatever his professed stylistic and esthetic allegiances.

5) That for all these reasons Stravinsky was the most completely Russian composer of art music that ever was and, if present trends continue, that ever will be.

Exerpted from the forthcoming *Stravinsky and the Russian Traditions* by Richard Taruskin, with permission granted by the University of California Press (Berkeley and Los Angeles).

19

An Interview With Dmitri Pokrovsky

What's the status of Stravinsky in Russia today?

In 1929 Igor Glebov, the leader of official Soviet musicology, published an extensive analysis of Stravinsky as a contemporary Russian composer. Glebov related Stravinsky to Russian classical music and to folk music. So as early as 1929 Stravinsky was officially claimed as a great Russian composer. In 1948, Zdanov, the top Communist ideologist, criticized Stravinsky as a modernist — but as a *Russian* modernist, just like Prokofiev and Shostakovich. When I was a music student in Moscow in the early sixties, part of our curriculum was a survey course of great Russian composers. We studied Glinka, Borodin, Mussorgky, Rimsky-Korsakov, Tchaikovsky, Stravinsky, Prokofiev, and Shostakovich. Performances of Stravinsky's Russian pieces, especially *The Firebird* and *Petrushka,* were extremely popular at this time.

What about "The Rite of Spring"?

In the survey course, we only studied certain works. For Beethoven, we studied the Third, Fifth, and Ninth Symphonies. For Stravinsky, we didn't study *The Rite of Spring* — although of course we heard recordings of it. I would say that in Russia today the Russian-period pieces remain the most popular, the most accessible to the Russian sensibility. On the other hand, the *Symphony of Psalms* (1930) is also extremely popular. I would say that scores like *Apollo* (1928) and *Orpheus* (1947) are not well-known. The serial Stravinsky of the fifties and sixties, of course, is known to musicians — at the Moscow Conservatory today, you have to know serial music. But for audiences I wouldn't say it's any more or less popular than any other serial music.

What about "Les noces" and "Renard," both of which you perform at BAM?

Les noces has become pretty popular in Russia. The Moscow Chamber Opera, for instance, does it. *Renard* is less known.

In the West we mainly know Stravinsky as a cosmopolitan modernist. What's the Russian perspective on Stravinsky's roots in Russian culture?

For Russian musicologists Stravinsky is a critical part of Russian musical culture, and that includes the music he composed after leaving Russia in 1911. For instance, they include Stravinsky's neo-classical period, in the twenties, as part of the neo-classical movement in Russia. His avant-garde music is considered part of the Russian avant-garde. And contemporary musicologists believe that Russian folk music and folk oral traditions are inherent in all of Stravinsky's work. From an American perspective, it may seem significant which Russian composers or painters left Russia and which didn't leave. But for Russians, it's all the same. Kandinsky left, Malevich didn't leave — what's the difference? They both went through similar stylistic changes.

Village khorovod
(ceremonial dance),
from an anonymous 1857 broadside.

How did you come to undertake your Stravinsky research?

In 1973 I was hired to teach a course on the history of Russian instrumental music at the Gnessin Institute in Moscow. My research took me to folk influences on Glinka. This became the starting point for my research on the links between folk music and Russian composers. At that time, balalaika orchestras would perform Bach, Mozart, and Paganini and that was considered Russian folk art. Obviously, there was a conflict between the instruments and the music. And then I found that the orchestras were also false — because you cannot find such a balalaika orchestra in any Russian village. It was a nationalistic creation that had nothing to do with either classical music or folk music. It was an attempt, beginning with Tsar Nicholas II, to create an artificial Russian folk culture on the level of Western classical culture. And this was around the time that Stravinsky started his folk music research. So when we talk about what Stravinsky heard around him and what conventions he tried to escape — he tried to escape this, too. In between Stravinsky and Russian folk culture was this artificial folk culture.

Are you, in effect, crossing a barrier he never crossed?

He actually crossed the barrier himself. The biggest surprise to me, in my research into rural folk music, was that Stravinsky obviously knew the differences between melodic patterns in different parts of a village wedding ceremony. He obviously came into contact with authentic oral tradition. Unlike Bartók in Hungary, he never undertook expeditions to the countryside specifically to collect folk tunes. But he definitely encountered authentic folk singers, and transcribed what he heard. We know that he visited parts of southern and western Russia around the turn of the century, and I am certain that the musical style of these regions was in his ear when he composed *Les noces*. He wasn't just quoting folk

songs he found in collections, the way Rimsky-Korsakov did. And, unlike Rimsky and other previous nationalist composers, Stravinsky understood that folk singers don't perform "songs" with fixed melodies. What they do is combine short musical cells, and also short segments of text. And these combinations and recombinations are spontaneous and unrehearsed. Stravinsky did this exactly: he combined and recombined different musical and text patterns. The libretto for *Les noces* is like a traditional song, full of abrupt juxtapositions. And, as I said, different parts of the wedding ceremonies Stravinsky adapted in *Les noces* use different melodic patterns.

How did you come to discover this?

At the beginning of the 1970s Shostakovich encouraged field research into the real sound of Russian folk music. Money was made available for expeditions. And that's when I became a young folklore enthusiast. My teacher in St. Petersburg, Professor Yevgeny Hippius, was a student of Bartók. Previously, I had intended to become a conductor. I abandoned that. I only wanted to be able to produce the sounds which I heard in rural Russia. So I started to research singing techniques — the voice as a musical instrument. I reconnected to Stravinsky only in 1982. The year before, I had visited the village where Mussorgsky was born, and recorded songs Mussorgsky used in his opera *Khovanshchina*. So I got the idea that composers are influenced by music that they heard in their early childhood. But with Stravinsky, this went nowhere, since he was born in a suburb of St. Petersburg. This was a problem for me for a long, long time. I only found a solution when I began field research based on the text of *Les noces*. This took me to Smolensk, Kaluga, and Belgorod in western Russia, and Ust-Luge in the Ukraine.

As an outgrowth of your ethnomusicological research into the source materials for Stravinsky's works, you've now undertaken to conduct the Stravinsky pieces themselves, but in a performance style informed by your knowledge of oral tradition. As a result, your Stravinsky performances sound much different from anyone else's, including the performances Stravinsky himself conducted and recorded. What would he have made of this?

Stravinsky was a pretty complicated person. But I'm pretty sure if he heard our *Les noces* he would definitely confirm that it resembles what he heard in his ear. And I know he was never happy with any performances of *Les noces*.

Nicolas Roerich, design for *The Rite of Spring*, first tableau.

Why do you use mechanical pianos in "Les noces"?

Stravinsky himself described *Les noces* as "perfectly homogeneous, perfectly impersonal, and perfectly mechanical." He was fascinated with the mechanical reproduction of sound. When he was working out the scoring of *Les noces*, one of the ensembles included a pianola, or mechanical piano. Stravinsky liked the sound of the pianola, but there were difficulties synchronizing it with acoustic instruments. We've recreated the piano parts of *Les noces* on an Apple Macintosh. In my opinion, this solution may well have appealed to Stravinsky had it been available to him.

We haven't yet mentioned your research on "The Rite of Spring."

The Rite of Spring was influenced by Russia a lot. But in *The Rite of Spring* Stravinsky doesn't use the folk techniques you find in *Renard* and *Les noces*. He uses melodies, just like his teacher Rimsky-Korsakov. And he mostly takes them from published sources. He doesn't even care that the melodies have nothing to do with the pagan rituals they accompany in the ballet.

Do your reseach and conclusions parallel Richard Taruskin's?

Yes. But in my opinion Stravinsky was more of a folklorist than Taruskin seems to believe. Stravinsky didn't create compositional theories of the kind Bartók created as a result of his field research. But I'm sure Stravinsky transcribed folk music just as Bartók did. Taruskin sees Stravinsky absorbing folk tradition more indirectly; he talks about him "fabricating authentic folklore." I speak of the ethnographically accuracy of Stravinsky because Stravinsky precisely follows the oral rules that folk singers use. These rules are different according to regional styles. They are different inside the same regional style in different genres. And they are slightly different in the same genre, such as wedding songs, according to the position in the ritual. I mean, if something's sung to the father of the bride, it has one melodic pattern. If it's sung to the bride, it has an absolutely different pattern. And Stravinsky followed these differences in microscopic detail. That's what we found out. That was amazing.

Also, I don't agree with Richard that Stravinsky used the musical style of lament in *Les noces* (see page 57). The opening "lament" is not a lament but a wedding song with a text about lamenting. The melodic pattern, scale, and rhythm of this song are very well preserved in *Les noces*. Only in one region of Russia do laments use some of the same elements as this song.

And Richard finds "anti-humanist" implications in the communal rituals of "Les noces."

After so many years of Soviet rule, I'm uncomfortable with this kind of interpretation. Stravinsky was influenced by the philosophy of his time not to apply his own societal rules to the customs of societies based on mythological consciousness. Perhaps his presentation of *Les noces* and *The Rite of Spring* was not so "anti-humanist," but rather a desire to present an unbiased view.

Taruskin says Stravinsky was embarrassed by his Russian past, that he suffered from a sense of cultural inferiority, that his reminiscences falsify his creative history.

I think that's all true. I would look for reasons not in Russia but in France. In Paris, Stravinsky had to be a successful composer and to be Russian at the same time. That was hard. I was just visiting the Museum of Modern Art in New York, and discovered that Kandinsky was a "French painter born in Russia." I was shocked by this. But it's so familiar, if you think about Stravinsky.

STRAVINSKY AND RUSSIAN VISUAL ART

Russian visual art is remarkably little known in the United States. Even such a towering figure as Ilya Repin, the leading Russian painter of the late nineteenth century, remains obscure (although we have often seen his magnificent portrait of Mussorgsky without realizing who painted it). It follows that Stravinsky's relationship to Russian art is equally unrecognized. Of the two essays that follow, the first, by Elizabeth Kridl Valkenier, recounts the birth of a national style, beginning in the 1860s — a development including Repin, and paralleling the nationalism of Stravinsky's teacher Rimsky-Korsakov. The second essay, by John E. Bowlt, considers the further evolution of neo-nationalism and neo-primitivism within Sergei Diaghilev's Mir isskustva — a circle of painters and writers of which Stravinsky was part.

The Birth of National Style

by Elizabeth Kridl Valkenier

The *Peredvizhniki* (or "Wanderers") were realist painters of the second half of the nineteenth century. Rejecting the neo-classicism of the Imperial Academy of Arts, which promoted paintings of scenes from the bible and classical history, they were the first to achieve the dignity of high art for distinctly Russian subject matter, and thus to imprint on it a national idiom. Their strivings and accomplishment created the seedbed from which further genuine national expression — not just in content but also in style — could grow at the turn of the century, with the advent of Diaghilev, Stravinsky, and *Mir isskustva*.

Russian realism was born in the 1860s. This was the decade when serfdom was abolished, a system of local self-government was organized, and the judicial system was reformed. Autocracy conceded some of its prerogatives and rigid societal bonds were loosened. It was a decade of reform and renovation which left no facet of national life unchanged.

The fine arts, too, were caught up in the ferment. Here the sources of change were several. The liberal public rejected the Italianesque neo-classicism promoted by the Imperial Academy, for it represented the autocratic regime's lack of concern for the lives and needs of common people. Moscow's rising middle class wanted to assert its own cultural values, distinct from those of cosmopolitan St. Petersburg. The young generation of painters wanted to establish their professional independence and dignity. Spurring them on was one of those irascible Russian intellectuals, the critic Vladimir Stasov, who devoted his pen to the defense and promotion of a new national art. Nor should it be forgotten that the quest for nationally identifiable art was sweeping the rest of Europe at the time.

The confluence of these trends led to the formation in 1870 of the first independent exhibiting society — the Association of Traveling Art Exhibits; the founding of the first art gallery devoted exclusively to

Russian art, by the Moscow textile merchant Pavel Tretiakov; and endless, passionate discussions about the appropriate content and style for Russian art.

At the outset, an activist, civic-minded trend prevailed. Historical canvases, portraiture, and social genre called attention to the government's backsliding in reforms, the bureaucracy's corruption, the ubiquitous social inequalities. But already then some thoughtful objections were raised, notably by the ethnographer Fedor Buslaev; he argued that medieval Russian architecture and folklore, not topical socio-political subjects, should be the appropriate source for genuine national art.

Similarly, already during the first decade of the Traveling Exhibits, canvases based on Russian folk themes already appeared together with politically inspired disquisitions on the contemporary peasantry and their lot. Ivan Kramskoy, the founder and acknowledged philosopher of the Association, exhibited the canvas "May Night" — a poetic scene, drawn from folk legend, of nymphs in moonlight — in the first show of 1871, where it hung alongside Nikolai Ge's "Peter I and Alexis." The latter, showing the confrontation of reformist father and retrogressive son, was a graphic reminder of the need to press on with changing Russia.

In the next decade, the 1880s, individual painters with a broader vision of the national heritage emerged on the scene. Vasili Surikov and Viktor Vasnetsov celebrated the beauty of medieval Russia unaffected by Peter the Great's Westernizing reforms. Mikhail Nesterov depicted the spiritual intensity of the Russian Orthodox Church a well as the beatitudes of its numerous saints.

By the 1890s the creative impulse of the *Peredvizhniki* ran dry. The painters' success had ossified into a chauvinistic and inflexible group identity, known as *Peredvizhnichestvo*. Simultaneously, the *Peredvizhniki* were coopted by Alexander III. The Tsar set up in St. Petersburg a Russian Art Museum to rival Moscow's Tretiakov Gallery, and in effect enlisted *Peredvizhnichestvo* in the government's efforts to create an official Russian nationalism.

No longer attracting fresh talent, the Association tried to dominate the artistic scene by refusing membership to those artists who deviated from painting recognizably Russian scenes in a straightforward naturalistic manner. This was the situation that provoked Diaghilev and *Mir iskusstva* to mount their challenge.

However, not all the realists fitted into the straitjacket of *Peredvizhnichestvo*. Ilya Repin (1844-1930) was the most talented and celebrated member of the Association, whose dramatic pictures enlivened the Traveling Exhibits from 1878 on and caused as much comment as Tolstoy's writings. Repin resisted the imposition of a programmatic Russian realism. He resigned from the Association, broke off with his lifelong friend and supporter Stasov, tried to reform the Academy of Arts and to inspire the young generation by sponsoring innovative shows of new trends, both Russian and foreign. The verve of his brush as well as his outspoken defense of free art (namely, that it should not resist change and be separated from the West by any patriotic "Chinese wall") were recognized and applauded by young artists. So much so that when Diaghilev in 1898 planned the publication of *Mir iskusstva* to prod the parochial Russian public

Ilya Repin, Portrait of Vladimir Stasov (1883). The Russian Museum, St. Petersburg.

Karl Briullov, "The Last Day of Pompeii" (1830-33). The Russian Museum, St. Petersburg.

out of its isolation, he invited Repin to serve on the journal's editorial board and intended to devote one of its first issues to Repin's work. Unfortunately, a quarrel took place which — given the highly charged politics of Russian art — quickly assumed the dimensions of fundamental ideological-philosophical-aesthetic dis-

Ilya Repin,
"The Zaporozhya Cossacks"
(sketch, 1880s).
The Russian Museum, St. Petersburg.

agreement. In consequence, for the rest of his life Repin was pigeonholed (and often acted) as the spokesman for the intolerant *Peredvizhnichestvo* — with which, prior to this dispute with Diaghilev, he had never been identified.

Yet, neither Repin's nor the *Peredvizhniki's* contributions to making artists and the public sensitive to the beauties of native scenes and traditions should be overlooked, for they were the first to turn in that direction. And there is evidence that Stravinsky appreciated this legacy early in his career.

In 1911 Stravinsky wrote a letter to Rimsky-Korsakov's son, expressing reverence for — and indebtedness to — the various strands that went into the creation of a Russian style in art. His tolerant attitude accepted innovators of both the nineteenth and twentieth centuries, and acknowledged the organic nature of cultural development. He objected to the "one-sided and noxious" identification of the Russian style with that of such *Mir isskustva* contemporaries as Ivan Bilibin and Nicolas Roerich. As far as he was concerned, Stravinsky continued, he valued just as much such *Peredvizhniki* as Repin, Vasili Perov, and Illarion Prianishnikov. He specified that his respect for the nineteenth-century realists in no way made the younger painters any less Russian, adding that the same open-minded approach should be used in judging his own musical works.

Stravinsky and Diaghilev's *Mir iskusstva*

by John E. Bowlt

To establish the relationship of Igor Stravinsky to the cultural ambience of fin-de-siécle Russia and, specifically, to Sergei Diaghilev's World of Art group (in Russian: *Mir iskusstva*) is no easy task. Even if we limit ourselves to *Mir iskusstva* as a journal (1898-1904) and exhibition society (1899-1906), we are still confronted with an extremely complex mosaic of literary, visual, and musical concepts. As Dmitri Filosofov, Diaghilev's cousin and the literary factotum of *Mir iskusstva*, argued, "the World of Art...was the cult of dilettantism in the good and true sense of the word." Alexandre Benois, the journal's practical editor, reinforced this opinion in his history of the group published in Leningrad in 1928:

> I consider that, by the "World of Art," we should understand not this, that or the other in isolation, but everything together, or rather, a kind of collective which lived its own distinctive life, which had its own interests and aims, which tried to influence society in various ways and to awaken in society a desired response to art.

Certainly, no history of the Russian Silver Age can be written without substantial reference to *Mir isskustva,* the more so since its direct and legitimate progeny was Diaghilev's Ballets Russes of 1909-29 to which, of course, Stravinsky contributed so much.

The primary members of the World of Art — Léon Bakst, Benois, Ivan Bilibin, Sergei Diaghilev, Mstislav Dobujinsky, Zinaida Gippius, Evgenii Lancéray, Dmitrii Merezhkovsky, Nicolas Roerich, and Konstantin Somov — were united neither by age nor by profession, neither by social status nor by emotional sensibility. And while they all resisted the weight of nineteenth century Realism, as represented by the *Peredvizhiniki,* their tastes ranged from ancient Greece (Bakst) to Versailles (Benois), from eighteenth century St. Petersburg (Lancéray) to pagan Slavdom (Roerich), and their intellectual gatherings were marked more by dissent and rivalry than by unanimity of purpose — something that we sense in a letter that Benois wrote to the poet Merezhkovsky in 1903:

> Whatever you say, for you the history of the world is coming to an end....But our attitude is quite different. For us, the world — despite triumphant Americanism, railroads, telegraphs, telephones, all this modern brutality and vulgarity, all this despicable transformation of the *earth* — for us the world still contains great enchantment and, most important, is full of promise.

Such contradictions were no less characteristic of the Ballets Russes later on. We think, for example, of the tense, polemical environment in which Stravinsky completed *Petrushka* in 1911:

Nicolas Roerich painting the apse of the Talashkino estate church, 1880s.

Fokine found the rhythms for the ensembles unjustifiably complicated; Benois resented the threatened interference of Leon Bakst; Diaghilev wanted the score to end on a major chord; Stravinsky insisted that it close on an unfinished phrase.

There are many obvious parallels between Stravinsky's major exploits and *Mir isskustva*, apart from his personal proximity to Diaghilev. That *The Firebird (Zhar-ptitsa)* was one of the World of Art's favorite fairy-tales is clear, for example, from Bilibin's sumptuous illustrations to the 1899 de luxe edition of *The Tale of Ivan-Tsarevich, the Fire-Bird and the Grey Wolf,* from Konstantin Bal'mont's cycle of poems *Zhar-ptitsa* (Moscow, 1907), and from the title of the Berlin journal (*Zhar-ptitsa*) of 1921-26 that so many of the World of Art artists and writers supported in emigration. *Petrushka* was a narrative that Benois connected fondly with his childhood experiences of the *balagany* (fairground booths) in St. Petersburg and that relates to the entire pierrotic cult among the Symbolists — from Alexander Blok's *Balaganchik* to Somov's Harlequinades.

The Rite of Spring is a particular example of this cross-fertilization of ideas, since it owed much to the ethnographical studies of its designer, Roerich, and to the vast folklore collection that Princess Mariia Tenisheva (co-sponsor of the journal *Mir iskusstva*) amassed at her estate, Talashkino, in the early twentieth century — an artistic retreat that attracted Bilibin, Sergei Maliutin, Mikhail Vrubel, and other associates of the World of Art as well as Stravinsky himself. At Talashkino, Roerich felt that he had rediscovered an organic connection with the indigenous traditions of ancient Russia — and no doubt he remembered the workshops for woodcarving, embroidery, and balalaikas, when he designed his sets and costumes for *The Rite of Spring.*

These connections have received some attention on the part of researchers, and the perimeters of those cultural territories have been charted and assessed, especially in the case of *The Rite of Spring.* However, there are other less familiar junctures in the intricate network that joined Bakst, Andrei Bely, Benois, Blok, Diaghilev, Somov, Stravinsky, Vrubel, and other representa-

tives of Russia's Silver Age, especially within the framework of the World of Art. Of particular importance here was the nucleus of the Russian Symbolist philosophers — Belïy, Gippius, Viacheslav Ivanov, Merezhkovsky, and Vasilii Rozanov — all of whom contributed essays to *Mir iskusstva,* and examination of their writings helps us to understand some of Stravinsky's own musical attitudes and resolutions. Even though these philosophers emphasized different concepts, their intellectual elaborations derived from a common denominator or set of emphases. They agreed with Diaghilev, for example, that the artist's prerogative was individual expression and that

> for anyone perceiving the work of art, the
> value and meaning of it is to be found in
> the most vivid manifestation of the creator's
> individuum.

They were also convinced that Russia was on the threshold of a cultural renaissance "for we are greater and broader than anyone"; and that art and literature would be regenerated through a return to archaic and primordial conditions. Judging from Stravinsky's early ballets, this aspiration was fundamental to his creativity, as well.

Perhaps the most vital argument that the Symbolists discussed on the pages of *Mir iskusstva* concerned the privileged status of music — an argument that must have impressed the young Stravinsky. The role of music in the World of Art society in general has not received close scrutiny, (although Grigorii Bernardt's book on Benois and music and now Richard Taruskin's synthetic study of Stravinsky can be recommended as pioneering contributions to the subject). Though the World of Art is remembered largely as an artistic, theatrical, and literary contingent, its interest in music was professional and provocative, touching on familiar topics such as Wagner and the operatic drama as well as more esoteric concerns. Diaghilev was an avid concert-goer and we remember him for his attendance at Wanda Landowska's soirée in Moscow in 1897 and the concert of Russian and Finnish music at the Helsinki Atheneum in 1898, for his organization of the Concerts of Russian Music for the Salon d'Automne in Paris in 1906, and, of course, for his creation of the Ballets Russes. Diaghilev

Fedor Shekhtel,
Staircase in the Riabushinsky Villa,
Moscow (1900-02).

Nicolas Roerich,
"Idols" (1901).
The Russian Museum, St. Petersburg.

himself contended that his esthetic taste had been nurtured by "Giotto, Shakespeare and Bach, the greatest gods of our artistic mythology...and with them Puvis de Chanvannes, Dostoevsky, and Wagner." Diaghilev's World of Art colleague Alfred Nourok was responsible for the Evenings of Contemporary Music in St. Petersburg between 1901 and 1912.

Although the *Mir isskustva* taste in contemporary music was eclectic — Delibes, Grieg, Nikolai Medtner, Rebikov, Rimsky-Korsakov, Scriabin — the group was united in its conception of music as an elevated medium of expression that "dominated the other arts." For the Symbolists in general music was the "radiant daughter of dark chaos" and the "soul of all the arts" and they invested music with a cathartic and therapeutic quality that, they felt, could ennoble and transform mankind. In this sense they regarded Wagner and Scriabin as principal components of their contemporary renaissance in contradistinction to the "decadents" of twentieth century bourgeois society. In Diaghilev's opinion, "sentimental sighers fading away to the sounds of Mendelsohn *Lieder* "were quite capable of listening to *Pagliacci* one moment and the *Nibelungen* the next."

In other words, to the World of Art members music was more than "music". Belïy made this

clear in his article "Formy iskusstva" [The Forms of Art] published in *Mir iskusstva* in 1902, in which he constructed a hierarcy of the arts, asserting that the literary and visual arts were "empirical" and "physical" and should aspire towards the immateriality of music:

The evolution of the world of art is from architecture to symphonic music. Historically and in a temporal sequence music was formed later, but in a formal sequence it is the perfect art. In removing the material of the arts, it is the figured-bass of all the arts and the first seed of the art of the future.

Belïy's philosophical justification of a musical primacy coincided with many discussions of related subjects on the pages of *Mir iskusstva* and other journals of the Silver Age such as *Zolotoe runo* [Golden Fleece] and *Apollon* [Apollo] and was reflected in Bal'mont's enthusiasm for Scriabin, Ivanov's investigations into the musical painting of the Lithuanian Mikolajaus Ciurlionis, and Belïy's implication that there is an inherent link between the seven colors of the spectrum and the seven notes of the diatonic scale. Belïy's recognition of the "approach of inner music to the surface of the consciousness" brings to mind Vasilii Kandinsky's evocation of the "inner sound" in painting and the musical

parallels of his *Improvisations* (we remember that Kandinsky was also a contributor to *Mir iskusstva*). In broader terms, the endowment of music with a spiritual or "fleshless" energy might have served as a principal stimulus to the entire notion of abstraction and non-objectivity explored by the avant-garde painters in the 1910s.

As far as Stravinsky is concerned, perhaps the "cosmic" dimension that the Symbolists identified with music was less important than their parallel emphasis on rhythm and their explication of rhythm as the dynamic and integratory motif of culture. They considered an essential property of music to be not the "tune" (which might be descriptive or programmatic), but rhythm. Whether in a symphony, a poem, a painting, or even a piece of architecture (Fedor Shekhtel's sinuous *art nouveau* houses), rhythm was regarded as a connective device, intuitive, primordial and constant. This sentiment was encountered again and again even after Symbolism had ceased to exist as a identifiable movement. For example, the poet and philosopher Blok identified the October Revolution as the extension of natural kinetics whose "musical strainings" had already been heeded by Wagner:

> The entire complexity of poetical and musical rhythms...is nothing but the musical preparation of a new cultural movement, the reflection of those elemental and natur-

al rhythms which have form the overture to the epoch opening before us.

Of course, the "elemental and natural rhythms" are among the most striking qualities of Stravinsky's music, akin to the "a-rhythm...asymmetry...and a-harmony" that Kandinsky identified with modern art. In this context, too, we can understand why the radical "neo-primitivist" artists Natalia Goncharova and Mikhail Larionov, were closer to the fin-de-siècle than they might have admitted. The leaders of Moscow's brash and boisterous avant-garde before the First World War, they directed their commitment to Diaghilev and the Ballets Russes.

It might seem a paradox that Goncharova and Larionov, with their outrageous exhibitions, their involvement in civic and judicial scandals, their face-painting, and — in the words of one contemporary observer — their "brazen can-can in the temple of art," should have rushed to join the prim, if not proper, Diaghilev in Paris. But their collaboration can be explained precisely through the Symbolist's emphases on the indigenous, the archaic, and the "rhythmical." Goncharova and Larionov brought a new energy and vitality to the professional stage through their passion for the primitive — icons, peasant embroideries, signboards, graffiti, wooden toys, and *lubki* (handcolored prints). As they declared in 1913: "Simple, uncorrupted people are closer to us than the artistic husk that clings

Natalia Goncharova,
"Washerwomen" (1911).
The Russian Museum, St. Petersburg

Natalia Goncharova,
"Peasants" (1911).
The Russian Museum, St. Petersburg.

to modern art like flies to honey." Their key assignments for Diaghilev expressed these basic assumptions, for *Coq d'or* (1914), *Soleil du minuit* (1915), *Les noces* (1923), and *Renard* (1922, 1929) relied substantially on "archaic" or, at least, traditional sources of inspiration. Goncharova and Larionov also discovered an "a-rhythm...asymmetry...and a-harmony" here and transferred the inverted perspective, bright colors, rude outlines, and rich ornament that they found in *lubki*, icons, and children's art to their studio paintings and theater sets. After Bakst,

Goncharova and Larionov were Diaghilev's greatest innovators in scenic design — and they looked forward precisely because they looked backward.

Without the acute sensibility of Diaghilev's *Mir isskustva*, without the legacy of its artistic pre-science and firm belief in the new, it is doubtful whether these artists or Stravinsky would have achieved the transformations that they did.

32

BROOKLYN PHILHARMONIC ORCHESTRA

Dennis Russell Davies, Principal Conductor
Lukas Foss, Conductor Laureate
40th Season, 1993/94

The Russian Stravinsky

BAM Opera House
May 6, 8 PM

DENNIS RUSSELL DAVIES, conductor

Pre-concert presentation at 7 pm: **Elizabeth Kridl Valkenier** on the *Peredvizhniki* and late nineteenth century Russian painting

NIKOLAI RIMSKY-KORSAKOV Suite from *Le Coq d'or* (1907)

IGOR STRAVINSKY *Scherzo fantastique* (1907-08)

Intermission

IGOR STRAVINSKY *The Firebird* (1909-10): two excerpts

1. Dance of the Firebird
2. Magic-Carillon—Appearance of Kashchei's Guardian Monsters—Capture of Ivan Tsarevich—Arrival of Kashchei—His Dialogue with Ivan—Intercession of the Princesses—Appearance of the Firebird—Dance of Kaschei's Retinue—Infernal Dance

ALEXANDER SCRIABIN *The Poem of Ecstasy* (1908)

Post-Concert Discussion with
Dennis Russell Davies, Joseph Horowitz, Dmitri Pokrovsky, Henry Schuman, Richard Taruskin, Elizabeth Kridl Valkenier

THE STANLEY H. KAPLAN EDUCATIONAL CENTER ACOUSTICAL SHELL
The Brooklyn Philharmonic and the Brooklyn Academy of Music gratefully acknowledge the generosity of Mr. and Mrs. Stanley H. Kaplan, whose assistance made possible the Stanley H. Kaplan Educational Center Acoustical Shell.

After Fyodor Stravinsky died in 1902, his son Igor, age 20, became closely attached to Nikolai Rimsky-Korsakov. He attended weekly musical gatherings at Rimsky's home. From the fall of 1905, he took regular private composition lessons from Rimsky-Korsakov until the latter's death in 1908. His early — and obscure — music is obviously indebted to that of his teacher. For the purposes of tonight's concert, Rimsky-Korsakov's well-known suite to his opera, Le Coq d'or (1907), is a convenient point of reference; its fairy tale enchantment suffuses Stravinsky's Scherzo fantastique (1907-08), which we also hear this evening. In fact, as Richard Taruskin notes, the Stravinsky of Scherzo fantastique is no less an exotic story-teller than is Rimsky in his operas and tone poems.

In this context, The Firebird (1909-10) is a transitional work. The idea of the firebird is folkloric — and so points toward Stravinsky's nationalism to come. And yet this ballet score, which mimes stage action in exquisite detail, clings to the musical world of Rimsky. According to Taruskin, Stravinsky's later contention that he composed The Firebird "in revolt against poor Rimsky" is unsupportable; not until The Rite of Spring did Stravinsky finally attain a convincing fusion of modernism and folklore.

The Firebird, moreover, samples the soundworld of Alexander Scriabin (1872-1915), who was not a folklorist. The spangled musical trajectories of Scriabin's Poem of Ecstasy (1908) seemingly rematerialize in the "Dance of the Firebird" — the first of two extracts from the complete ballet we hear tonight.

Notes on the Program

by Richard Taruskin

Its eighty-year career as an international classic makes *Firebird* (*Zhar-ptitsa* in Russian) hard to see for the anomaly it was. This very self-consciously "Russian" work had no antecedent in Russian art and was expressly created for a non-Russian audience. And this was because Russian ballet before *Firebird* was actually French, and only the circumstances of its reimportation to France forced it to become Russian.

Faced with near bankruptcy after his first Parisian *saison russe* in 1909, at which both opera and ballet had been presented, Sergei Diaghilev recognized that the ballets had succeeded where the much more expensive operas had failed, and, "quite contrary to his own taste" (in the perhaps not quite ingenuous words of his chief adviser, the artist Alexandre Benois), the impresario decided to limit his Parisian presentations to the dance. But it had been the operas of 1909 (Glinka's *Ruslan and Ludmila*, Borodin's *Prince Igor*, Rimsky-Korsakov's *Maid of Pskov*) that had represented an authentic and, for the French, seductively exotic Russian art. (And henceforth, in the West, Russian art would have to be exotic in order to rank as authentic.) The ballets (*Les Sylphides*, *Le Pavillon d'Armide*, *Cléopâtre*) were all stylizations of the classical (that is, French) ballet, albeit executed on a level the French themselves could no longer match. Critics put Diaghilev on notice that if the Russian ballet was to continue to have a raison d'être in Paris, it would have to develop a repertory that could take the place of the operas that were no longer economically feasible, one that would deliver a musical *frisson* worthy of comparison with those administered by Diaghilev's dancers, designers, and choreographers.

Such a repertory did not exist. Before what Benois called Diaghilev's "export campaign," most of the creative force behind Russian ballet had been imported from the West. The genre had long been regarded by progressive artists and thinkers as an outmoded relic of the autocracy, an art for snobs and skirt chasers. With the glorious exception of Tchaikovsky, and latterly of Glazunov, the ballet had never attracted the best musical

Konstantin Somov, frontispiece to *Zhar-ptitsa* (The Firebird)
a collection of poems by Kristantin Balmont (1907).

minds in Russia. They associated it with empty divertissement, often forcibly interpolated, and with imported "specialist" composers (that is, hacks) like Ludwig Minkus, Cesare Pugni, and Riccardo Drigo. Rimsky-Korsakov, for example, swore to a correspondent that he would *never* write a ballet (the italics were his), for six reasons.

> 1) Because it is a degenerate art.
> 2) Because miming is not a full-fledged art form.
> 3) Balletic miming is extremely elementary and leads to a naive kind of symbolism.
> 4) The best thing ballet has to offer, dances, are boring, since the language of dance and the whole vocabulary of movement is extremely skimpy.
> 5) There is no need for good music in ballet.
> 6) Ballet music is usually performed in a sloppy, perfunctory way.

To the members of Diaghilev's *Mir iskusstva* circle, things looked rather different. Precisely because it had stood aloof from the main trends of serious art in nineteenth-century Russia, precisely because it *was* divertissement, precisely because it had remained true to aristocratic principles of "classical" stylization, the ballet was far less tainted than opera with the hated residue of realism and was uncompromised by the didactic and populist concerns that encumbered modern Russian literature. The ballet was an inviting terrain for the kind of pure, untrammeled creative play that was the essence of the resurgent aristocratic art of the Russian "Silver Age," especially since the emergence of Mikhail Fokine, Diaghilev's reformist choreographer.

The choice of the Firebird as the subject for the work that would inaugurate a new pseudonationalist era in the Russian ballet was practically foreordained. As the paragon of benign magic and pure beauty in Russian folklore, the elusive, mercurial, radiant Firebird was the perfect metaphor of art itself as envisioned by the *Mir iskusstva* circle: the "light-winged, benevolent, free bird" of inspiration extolled by the poet Alexander Blok, striving for the rarefied, ecstatic creative bliss Scriabin extolled in his *Poem of Ecstasy*. It was no accident at all that Stravinsky modelled the dance symbolizing the Firebird's flight — the "Dance of the Firebird" we hear tonight, juxtaposed with *The Poem of Ecstasy* — on Scriabin's

harmonic style, or that he (unconsciously?) swiped a theme from Scriabin's score for this purpose —naturally, it was the one marked "volando" (flying).

There was no single Russian folktale or legend in which the *Firebird* was the central character. The scenario of the eventual ballet was worked out by Fokine on the basis of a bright idea that had been hit upon by Pyotr Potyomkin, a minor poet and balletomane whose entrée to the Diaghilev circle came by way of his being the lover of Walter Nouvel, the future ghostwriter of Stravinsky's autobiography. Probably recalling some verses by Yakov Polonsky that Russian schoolchildren still memorize, Potyomkin brought four stock folktale themes together: Firebird, Evil Sorcerer, Captive Princess, Prince Deliverer. The plot was pieced together out of two basic stories. "The Tale of Ivan-Tsarevich, the Firebird and the Grey Wolf," one of many tales published by the great nineteenth-century collector Alexander Afanasyev (whose books would later furnish the plots of Stravinsky's *Renard* and *Soldier's Tale*), was a typical quest narrative: Ivan-Tsarevich, the Russian "Prince Charming," seeks the Firebird with the magical assistance of the Grey Wolf and gains a captive princess for his bride into the bargain. In the ballet scenario, the Firebird, altogether out of character, combines the roles of quest-object and magical helper. The Evil Sorcerer (named Kashchey in many legends and in the scenario) came from a tale known as "The Self-Playing Zither" *(Gusli-samogudi)*, in which Ivan-Tsarevich finds the magic egg that contains the sorcerer's death, frees the princess, and weds her. From the beginning, it was assumed that the music for this ballet would be composed by Nikolai Tcherepnin (1873-1945), Diaghilev's staff conductor, who had already collaborated with Benois and Fokine on *Le Pavillon d'Armide*, one of the 1909 ballets. Tcherepnin actually began composing the score (a remnant survives in his tone poem, *The Enchanted Kingdom*) before falling out with Fokine and withdrawing. Next Diaghilev turned to Anatoly Lyadov, who declined despite an initial show of interest. (The well-known story that he accepted the commission but procrastinated is untrue.) Next Glazunov refused the offer. It was only after yet another composer, Nikolai Sokolov (1859-1922), had turned him down that Diaghilev, in desperation, approached the young

and relatively untested Igor Stravinsky, who was next in line, as it were, because Diaghilev had approached the five composers who had arranged the Chopin numbers for Fokine's 1909 Paris hit *Les Sylphides* one by one and in descending order of preference.

The fact that the new ballet was meant to replace opera in Diaghilev's programs, and thus by extension represented the continuation of Russian opera into the twentieth century, told mightily on its form and style. Lacking any immediate forebear in the classical Russian ballet, it took its place as heir to the long line of magic operas that began with Glinka's *Ruslan and Ludmila* and continued through the marvelous series by Rimsky-Korsakov, Stravinsky's teacher. The way in which Stravinsky contrasted the Russian folksong idiom associated with his human characters (Ivan-Tsarevich and the princesses) against the recondite harmonies of the fantastic ones (Kashchey, the Firebird) followed a convention established by Glinka some seventy years before. While Stravinsky modelled the benevolent, aerial magic of the *Firebird* on Scriabin's lofty and sensual idiom, the evil-sorcery harmonies are borrowed from Rimsky's longstanding practice. The Kashchey music is based on a "magic ladder" of alternating major and minor thirds, related to a scale of alternating whole and half steps that had fascinated Rimsky-Korskaov beginning with the opera *Sadko* (1896), whose very opening strikingly foreshadows the opening of *Firebird*, and which reached its Rimskian peak in an opera entitled *Kashchey the Deathless* (1902; revised 1906), which stands, both in subject and in musical technique, as a kind of parent to his pupil's ballet. When it came to writing the climactic "Danse infernale," moreover, Stravinsky's memory treacherously disguised itself as imagination and offered him the main theme of the analogous "hellish Kolo" from Rimsky-Korsakov's opera *Mlada*, in which Kashchey is also a character.

Rimsky-Korsakov's last opera, *The Golden Cockerel* (1907), also contains a lot of fiery birdsong, and also resonates, albeit not quite so directly, with the idiom of Stravinsky's *Firebird*. It was staged by Diaghilev in 1914, in a production so widely admired and imitated that its French title, *Le Coq d'or,* has been the opera's standard name in the West ever since. What made the production so influential was the spectacular gimmick, devised by Benois, of splitting the roles between dancers onstage, who mimed the action, and offstage singers who supplied the vocal parts as a sort of disembodied accompaniment. This gave Stravinsky the idea for his great trio of ballets with singing: *Les noces, Renard*, and *Pulcinella.*

But even without singing, no ballet has ever behaved more like an opera than *Firebird.* That is to say, no ballet ever featured a more regular, consistent, and dramaturgically effective alternation of mimed and danced episodes — exactly like operatic recitative and aria. The music that Stravinsky composed for the mimed episodes — in which he was guided at every turn by Fokine, whose movements he followed, improvising at the keyboard in the early stages of work — comes off very much like a kind of instrumental recitative, particularly in the confrontation between Ivan Tsarevich and Kashchey. The long section of mime beginning with the Magic Carillon and ending with the Infernal Dance, included in our program, is (except for the Infernal Dance itself) at once the least familiar music in *Firebird* (since it is not part of any of the popular suites the composer later drew from the score), and also the most original — the only part that gives any hint of the Stravinsky ballets that were to follow.

*　*　*

The *Scherzo fantastique,* completed in the spring of 1908, was the last work of Stravinsky's that Rimsky-Korsakov knew, and it is a veritable primer of the harmonic techniques Stravinsky learned from his teacher, techniques the critic Boris Asafyev aptly summed up as "the modest, rationalized impressionism of the St. Petersburg school," and which Stravinsky, far less charitably, wrote off in later years as "a few flimsy enharmonic devices." But then, Stravinsky's equivocations with respect to this particular piece are the best guide we have to his determination in later life to distance himself from the Russian milieu in which he had come of age, and repudiate its relevance to his later career. By now it is well established that, despite the composer's flat latterday denials (documented in page 15 in this booklet), the *Scherzo fantastique* was inspired by, and

Nikolai Rimsky-Korsakov

Alexander Scriabin

illustrated, passages in Maurice Maeterlinck's *Vie des abeilles* (known in English as *The Life of the Bee*). Once one knows this, the correspondences between the music and the literary source fairly leap to the ear.

The very opening of the piece, to begin with—a four-note leitmotif given out by a muted trumpet playing *forte*, as thin and piercing a timbre as can be imagined—could only have been suggested by this passage from Maeterlinck's fourth chapter ("The Young Queens"): ". . . and at last she goes, and wanders from comb to comb, her unsatisfied wrath finding vent in the war-song, or angry complaint, that every bee-keeper knows; resembling somewhat the note of a *distant trumpet of silver;* so intense, in its passionate feebleness, as to be clearly audible, in the evening especially, two or three yards away from the double walls of the most carefully enclosed hive." Maeterlinck goes on immediately to note the "magical effect" this song has on the worker bees, and in Stravinsky's *Scherzo* the opening trumpet call is followed by the first "magical" harmonies, a complete whole-tone scale built up out of successive rushing entrances in the strings, and ending in a pulsating *tremolando:* we hear worker after worker coming to attention.

The "A" section of this traditional A-B-A scherzo, in all its perpetual-motion scurry and bustle, obviously represents "The Swarm," so entrancingly described by Maeterlinck in his second chapter. Passages of sequential patterning around octatonic or whole tone progressions, their elements recurring in a predictable periodicity, give an ineluctable impression of circularity. (Such things, in fact, are usually called harmonic "circulations" or "rotations" in the technical literature; the term "octatonic" refers to an eight-tone scale of alternating tones and semitones that fascinated Rimsky-Korsakov and all his pupils.) What better opportunity, then, to set the magic octatonic wheels a-spinning, than Maeterlinck's description of the motion of the swarm: ". . . they all seem bewitched; they fly in dense circles round and round, like a living jelly stirred by an invisible hand." The slower middle section (*Moderato assai*) of the *Scherzo* describes the queen bee's "Nuptial Flight" *(Le Vol Nuptial),* as described in Maeterlinck's fifth chapter. The treacly erotic music of this section is always compared with

Wagner, though exactly what Wagner seems to be anyone's guess: *Tannhäuser, Meistersinger, Parsifal* have all been put forth as candidates. The Wagnerian resonance was not Stravinsky's idea, however. What musician of the early twentieth century could have read the following passage from Maeterlinck and not thought of *Tristan?*

> Prodigious nuptials, these, the most fairy-like that can be conceived, azure and tragic, raised high above life by the impetus of desire; imperishable and terrible, unique and bewildering, solitary and infinite. An admirable ecstasy, wherein death, supervening in all that our sphere has of most limpid and loveliest, in virginal, limitless space, stamps the instant of happiness on the sublime transparence of the great sky; purifying in that immaculate light the something of wretchedness that always hovers around love, rendering the kiss one that can never by forgotten.

Maeterlinck's description of the eventual apiarian *Liebestod* (the male's) must be an example of what Stravinsky had in mind when he wrote to Rimsky-Korsakov, "at first I thought that for the fullest exposition of the program I'd select definite citations from [Maeterlinck's] work, but I see that this will be impossible, since the language of science and of literature are too closely intertwined."

These are only a few of the most obvious and incontestable correspondences between Maeterlinck's poeticized prose and Stravinsky's imaginal music. They are enough to show how thoroughly the *Scherzo fantastique* was shaped by its literary source: elements from almost every chapter of the book play a part, and control the composition at every level. Stravinsky's music is not so much narrative or descriptive as metaphorical—which is probably why, ultimately, he felt it desirable to dispense with the program. Its publication might have spared him some complaints about the scherzo's harmonic audacities, and certainly about its length. In the end, though, he must have considered (or been persuaded) that a literalistic programmatic exterior might impede penetration of the interior world of feeling, and in this he already shows some Symbolist tendency. (Mallarmé: "Paint not the thing but the effect it produces.")

BROOKLYN PHILHARMONIC ORCHESTRA

Dennis Russell Davies, Principal Conductor
Lukas Foss, Conductor Laureate

40th Season, 1993/94

The Russian Stravinsky

BAM Opera House
May 7, 8 PM

DENNIS RUSSELL DAVIES, Conductor
THE POKROVSKY ENSEMBLE Dmitri Pokrovsky, Director

Pre-concert lecture at 7 pm: **Richard Taruskin**

MIKHAIL GLINKA *Kamarinskaya* (1848)

MILY BALAKIREV *Overture No. 2 on Russian Themes* (1864, revised 1884)

Intermission

Folk sources for *The Rite of Spring*
The Pokrovsky Ensemble
Sergei Zhirkov, gusly
Michael Korzin, principal violinist

Including the Spring calendar rituals the Arrow, the Wall on
the Wall, and the Funeral of Kastrama

IGOR STRAVINSKY *The Rite of Spring* (1911-13)
Part One: The Adoration of the Earth
Introduction
Auguries of Spring
The Game of Abduction
Ceremonial Dance
Games of the Rival Clans
Procession of the Wise Elders
Adoration of the Earth
Dance of the Earth

Part Two: The Sacrifice
Introduction
Mystical Circles of the Young Girls
Glorification of the Chosen Victim
The Summoning of the Elders
The Action of the Elders
Sacrificial Dance

If The Firebird *still essentially inhabits the musical world of Rimsky,* The Rite of Spring *(1911-13) does not. It is a turning point in Stravinsky's accommodation to the Russian avant-garde, to Diaghilev, Mir isskustva, and neo-nationalism. Collaborating with the important Mir isskustva artist Nicolas Roerich, Stravinsky here attempted to attain a true picture of primitive life; only through adherence to archeological authenticity at the conceptual stage, the neo-nationalists believed, would stylistic innovation — what came to be called modernism — be validated.*

The tumultuous first performance of The Rite of Spring *took place on May 29, 1913, at Paris' Théâtre des Champs-Elysées. The company was Diaghilev's Ballets Russes. The choreographer was Vaslav Nijinsky, the designer Roerich, the conductor Pierre Monteux.*

As a prelude to The Rite of Spring *— and to its source materials, as recreated by the Pokrovsky Ensemble — we also hear* Kamarinskaya *(1848) by the "father of Russian music," Mikhail Glinka (1814-1857), and the second* Overture on Russian Themes *(1864, revised 1884) by Mily Balakirev (1837-1910). These early national and nationalist exercises differ from Stravinsky's neo-nationalism — a distinction paralleling differences between Ilya Repin and the Peredvizhniki, in the late nineteenth century, and the neo-nationalist artists of the pre-World War I decades.*

Notes on the Program

by R i c h a r d   T a r u s k i n

"**K**amarinskaya" (accent on the second syllable) is a dance song consisting of a cadential phrase of three bars over which fiddlers, guitarists, balalaika players, concertina players, horn ensembles, and village bands used to improvise ostinato variations by the mile to accompany strenuous, competitive male dancing at weddings and festivals. It takes its name from the Komaritsky district in southern Russia.

During a visit to Warsaw in 1848, Mikhail Ivanovich Glinka found himself seated at the piano one day, amusing himself by improvising variations on the Kamarinskaya ostinato Chopsticks-fashion, when all at once he discovered that he was playing another one of his favorite folk songs: "The wedding song 'From Beyond the Mountains High' [*Iz-za gor vïsokikh*], which I used to hear in the country," as he tells us in his memoirs. "All at once," he continued,

> my imagination took fire, and . . . I wrote a piece for orchestra under the title "A Wedding Song and a Dance Song." I can assure the reader that I was guided in composing this piece solely by my innate musical feeling, thinking neither of what goes on at weddings, nor of how our orthodox populace goes about celebrating, nor of how a drunk might come home late and knock on the door so that he might be let in.

For Glinka, in other words, the national coloring of his composition was no more than "*pittoresque*," to use the word he himself applied to the work in its final title. *Kamarinskaya* was one of three *Fantaisies pittoresques* that Glinka wrote under the spell of Berlioz and his music, with which Glinka had become acquainted in Paris in 1844-45. The other two—*Jota aragonesa* and *Recuerdos de Castilla*, better known as *Souvenir d'une nuit d'été à Madrid*—were, as was so typical of Glinka's predilectons, of Spanish national character. Clearly it was nationality, not nativism, that mattered to Glinka, as to so many artists of the early and mid-nineteenth century (including, notably, Berlioz himself with his *Marche hongroise* and his *Carnaval romain*). In instrumental contexts,

national coloring was an exotic element, even if native, approached as the source of musical enjoyment rather than programmatic or symbolic content. The point of Glinka's *Kamarinskaya* was not a portrayal or a celebration of Russian life but a pretext for brilliant orchestration built around a kind of abstract musical pun, a motivic relationship between the two folk tunes (first presented as a contrasting pair, forming the basis of a slow introduction and an allegro respectively) that is spelled out delightfully in the middle of the piece, where the one theme is subtly and unexpectedly transformed into the other in a feat of compositional legerdemain.

Glinka's intentions for this entertaining piece may have been modest, but after his death the *Kamarinskaya* lived on and became the very emblem of burgeoning Russian nationalism in music. Tchaikovsky wrote of it, in a phrase that has become a virtual dogma in his homeland, that the Russian symphonic school was "all in *Kamarinskaya,* just as the whole oak is in the acorn." The Soviet musicologist Victor Tsukkerman has traced the genetic evolution of that oak in a volume of some 500 pages. And yet Tchaikovsky's simile does not seem quite right; for it suggests a spontaneous, natural germination, while the growth of the *Kamarinskaya* tradition was very much a cultivation, carefully tended and pruned in its initial stages by Mily Balakirev, both as composer and, later, as leader of a group now known as the "Mighty Five."

Unlike Glinka, Balakirev was a genuine musical nationalist, eager to establish the Russian school as something independent from "Europe." He wrote two overtures on Russian themes (1858, 1864) in direct emulation of *Kamarinskaya.* The second and more ambitious of the two — which we hear — was published in 1869 under the programmatic title *1000 Years* (commemorating the quasi- legendary founding of the Russian state at Novgorod by the Varangian Prince Rurik in 862 A.D.). It was reissued in 1890 under the jingoistic title *Rus',* the ur-Slavic name of the country known in Balakirev's day (and newly again in ours) as *Rossiya,* Russia.

Unlike Glinka, Balakirev thought of his overture as programmatic, in a multiple and oddly contradictory way. As the composer's political and cul-

tural orientation mutated over the years from a progressive to a reactionary position, so did the program. In 1869 Balakirev attached to the work a quotation from an essay by the exiled liberal writer Alexander Herzen, identifying his music with Russia's awakening social conscience. By 1907, when a new edition of the revised score was published (the last to come out during the composer's lifetime), Balakirev wanted his music to be heard as a protest against "the fatal blow dealt all Russian religious and national aspirations by the reforms of Peter the Great."

Like Glinka, Balakirev wove his themes with great skill into clever motivic and contrapuntal webs. Unlike Glinka, who came upon the idea for his *fantaisie pittoresque* quite serendipitously, Balakirev went looking for themes to incorporate into a preconceived symphonic plan, and found them during a song-collecting expedition along the Volga in the summer of 1860. (He published a whole book of them, including the ones used in *Russia,* in 1866). Still more unlike Glinka, and with an irony he never appreciated, the avowed nationalist Balakirev sought to do battle with the Germanic establishment by beating it at its own game. Where Glinka's innocently entertaining piece had been cast in an original, once-only, and genuinely folk-like form (introduction and ostinato variations), Balakirev's aggressively nationalistic opus took the form of an impeccably Teutonic sonata-allegro. One of the folk songs, a wedding tune called "There was no wind, then all of a sudden it blew" *(Ne bilo vetru, vdrug navyanulo),* forms the basis of the slow introduction. A round dance called "I'm off to Constantinople" *(Podoydu vo Tsar'-gorod),* is the "first theme" of the sonata design, and another round dance, "Merry Kate, black-browed Kate" *(Katen'ka vesyolaya, Katya chernobrovaya)* functions as "second theme." For the closing theme or codetta, Balakirev used a beautiful melody of his own devising, written while vacationing in the Caucasus in 1863.

While Glinka's *Kamarinskaya* was a one-shot deal, Balakirev's overtures did indeed lay the cornerstone of a school. They were the objects of enthusiastic emulation by the other members of Balakirev's circle (most famously in Borodin's "symphonic picture" *In Central Asia*), and continued to resonate in the symphonies of

Mikhail Glinka

Glazunov, Arensky, Kallinikov, and other academic symphonists at the turn of the century. And
that was because it was Balakirev, not Glinka,
who had reconciled Russian thematic content
with what Mussorgsky called "German transi-
tions." By these efforts he made the soil of
Russian instrumental music fertile. Without him
the acorn might have remained an acorn. But
the oak Balakirev midwifed was very much a
hothouse growth. It took a Stravinsky, in his
willfully iconoclastic *Rite of Spring,* to overturn
Balakirev's classicizing example and reestablish
(in the "Dance of the Earth") a direct link with
Glinka.

* * *

Stravinsky called his third ballet *Vesna
svyashchennaya,* Russian for "Holy Spring." *Le
Sacre du printemps,* the title under which it was
first performed by the Ballets Russes (with choreography by Vaslav Nijinsky) on 29 May 1913,
was suggested by the painter Leon Bakst (at first
in the plural: "Les Sacres du printemps") after the
work had gone into production. It has become
the standard designation outside of Russia and
the basis for the English title, *The Rite of Spring,*
first used by the Diaghilev company in London
in 1921 in connection with the ballet's postwar
revival (with choreography by Leonid Massine).

Stravinsky conceived the work in the spring of
1910; composed it between September 1911 and
March 1913; endured the riotous fiasco of the
premiere (at which it was the distasteful choreography, far more than the music, that offend-
ed); experienced through it, shortly before his
thirty- second birthday in 1914, the triumph of
his career ("such as *composers* rarely enjoy," he
recalled in old age); and spent the rest of his

long life telling lies about it. In 1920 he told a
reporter that the ballet had been originally conceived as a piece of pure, plotless instrumental
music ("une oeuvre architectonique et non anec-
dotique"). In 1931 he told his first authorized
biographer that the opening bassoon melody
was the only quoted folk song in the score. In
1959 he asserted, through his musical and literary assistant Robert Craft, that the work was
wholly without tradition, the product of intuition
alone. "I heard and I wrote what I heard," he
declared. "I am the vessel through which *Le
Sacre* passed." These allegations and famous
words have passed into the enduring folklore of
twentieth-century music.

In fact, the ballet's scenario is a highly detailed
and (but for the culminating human sacrifice)
ethnographically accurate pair of "scenes of
pagan Russia," as the ballet's frequently sup-
pressed subtitle proclaims. It was planned in
painstaking detail, before a note was written, by
the composer in collaboration with the Russian
painter and archeologist Nicolas Roerich, to
whom the work is dedicated. The score contains
at least nine identifiable folk songs, all of them
selected with the same eye toward ethnographic
authenticity that governed the assembling of the
scenario. Finally, the music magnificently
embodies and extends the same immediate and
local tradition, based on novel manipulations of
what was known among St. Petersburg musicians
as the "Rimsky-Korsakov scale" (a regular alternation, first used by Liszt, of whole steps and
half steps), as did such earlier Stravinsky scores
as the *Scherzo fantastique, Fireworks,* and
Petrushka.

Stravinsky's mendacity was not the result merely

Mily Balakirev

of a faulty memory; but neither was it merely vain or cynical. Having renounced Russia in the wake of the Bolshevik coup d'état, Stravinsky wished frantically not only to attach himself to the Western musical mainstream, but also to become its leader. He zealously distanced himself from the parochial lore of his birthright and embraced an aggressively cosmopolitan ideology. Hence his insistence that his music— all his music—was "pure," abstract, (neo)classical, unbeholden to any specific time or place for its inspiration. And hence the legend of *The Rite* as a violent rupture with the past, when all the while it was an exuberantly maximalistic celebration of two pasts—the remote past of its subject and the more recent past of its style.

Pagan antiquity, meticulously reconstructed or imaginatively recreated, was a craze among the writers and artists of Russia during the tense period between the revolutions of 1905 and 1917. "In our hearts," wrote the poet Alexander Blok in 1908, "the needle of a seismograph has twitched." Over all sensitive spirits there lay a pall, "a relentless sense of catastrophe" that brought with it a consciousness of cultural impasse, of hopeless personal fragmentation and isolation—what a later poet would famously dub the "dissociation of sensibility." Blok drew a dark distinction between the "culture" *(kul'túra)* of the urban intelligentsia—artificial, rootless, materialist and rationalistic, and therefore bent on destruction—and the "elemental spontaneity" *(stikhi ya)* of the folk. The tragedy of modern man lay in his estrangement from the earth. It was the duty of artists to renounce "culture" and become "elemental people" who "see dreams and create legends, indivisible from the earth." To recapture this saving oneness one had to emulate the art and the attitudes of the peasant, who all unawares still practiced the ancient religion of the earth. "In our villages the maidens perform their khorovods, amuse themselves with games, sing their songs; they pose dark riddles, interpret dreams, weep over the deceased. Rituals, songs, khorovods, charms bring people close to nature, make them understand its nocturnal language, imitate its movements." Blok might already have been describing *The Rite of Spring.*

The leading poet-mythologist of the immediate pre-revolutionary period was Sergei

Scene from Stravinsky's *The Rite of Spring,* 1913. Costumes by Nicolas Roerich.

Mitrofanovich Gorodetsky, Stravinsky's almost exact contemporary, from whose first book, *Yar'* (1907), the fledgling composer had set two poems in the year of its publication. *Yar'* contained a group of poems headed "Yarilo," which is the name of the ancient Slavic sun god in summer, the season of his ascendency. In the first of these poems, a maiden priestess is hacked to death by an axe-wielding wizard in the process of carving an idol of Yarilo out of the trunk of a sacred linden tree. Not only does this poem foreshadow *The Rite's* theme of maiden sacrifice, it even supplies prototypes for two of the ballet's three solo *dramatis personae:* the Chosen One and the Oldest-and-Wisest. It is more than likely that this poem (along, perhaps, with Alexander Serov's old opera *Rogneda,* which contains a sacrifice scene, and in which Igor Stravinsky's father, the basso Fyodor Stravinsky, was a veteran performer) formed part of the immediate background to Stravinsky's fecundating "vision," which came to him as he was completing *The Firebird,* in which he saw an entranced virgin dancing herself to death in the presence of tribal wizards as sacrifice to the sun god.

Having had the idea, Stravinsky immediately sought out his eventual collaborator, for (as he put it in a letter to the editor of a St. Petersburg music magazine) "who could help me if not Roerich; who if not he is privy to the whole

Alexander Golovin, portrait of Nicolas Roerich.

secret of our forefathers' closeness to the earth?" Not only had Roerich already become famous for his archaistic paintings; he had published a sensational article the year before entitled "Joy in Art" *(Radost' iskusstvu),* which culminated in a lyrical neolithic fantasy that was virtually a readymade scenario:

> Let us take one last look at a scene of Stone Age life.... A holiday. Let it be the one with which the victory of the springtime sun was always celebrated. When all went out into the woods for long stretches of time to admire the fragrance of the trees: when they made fragrant wreaths out of the early greenery, and adorned themselves with them. When swift dances were danced, when all wished to please....The people rejoiced. Among them art was born. They were near to us. They surely sang. And their songs were heard beyond the lake and in all the islands. And great fires fluttered in yellow patches. Near them the crowd moved in dark spots. Waters, turbulent by day, have become calm and lilac-blue. And amid the nocturnal rejoicing the silhouettes of canoes glide swiftly on the lake.

Roerich's "holiday," combined with Stravinsky's "sacrifice," are already between them the whole embryo of *The Rite of Spring,* parts I and II respectively. In the ancient Slav agrarian religion the period of Yarilo's ascendency is bounded by two holidays: Semik, the festival of the thaw (falling, in terms of the later Christian calendar, on the seventh Thursday after Easter), at which auguries, fertility rites, and commemorations of the dead were performed; and Kupala, the midsummer festival (coinciding with St. John's Eve), at which animals were sacrificed while young people danced through fire and performed mating (bride-seizing) rituals. Roerich drew on descriptions of these rites in medieval Kievan chronicles and in the nineteenth-century folklorist Alexander Afanasyev's huge compendium *The Slavs' Poetic Outlook on Nature (Poèticheskiye vozzreniya slavyan na prirodu,* 1861-64), which contained a chapter devoted to "Folk Holidays." He also adapted some of Herodotus's descriptions of the rites of the ancient Scythians, predecessors of the Slavs over much of what is now southern Russia and the Central Asian republics of the so-called Commonwealth of Independent States. Finally, he made creative use of some then very recent research on the so-called *volkhvï,* folk magi who, acting as shamans, would whirl themselves into a trancelike state resembling death, and on their female soothsaying counterparts, thus deriving the role of the old woman who instructs the "adolescents" in the rites of augury at the very beginning of the ballet.

The scenario, planned in the summer of 1910, consisted of the following sections, titles of which can be found in the Stravinsky/Roerich correspondence and in the sketchbook Stravinsky began to fill up a year later, after finishing *Petrushka,* and after further consultations with Roerich on the estate of Princess Maria Tenisheva, a lavish patron of folk art who thus stood godmother to *The Rite:*

(Part I)
Introduction: Pipes
1. Divinations with wands, after Herodotus [="*Les Augures printaniers*" in the finished score]
2. Ceremonial dance [="*Rondes printanières*"]
3. Game of "Cities" after the Kievan Primary Chronicle (12th century) [="*Jeux des cités rivales*"]
4. "They Are Coming, They Are Bringing Him" [="*Cortège du Sage*"]
5. Game of Abduction, after the Primary Chronicle [="*Jeu du Rapt*"]
6. Wearing-Out of the Earth by Dancing [="*Danse de la Terre*"]

(Part II)
7. Ceremonial Dances, Secret Games, [="*Cercles mystérieux des Adolescentes*")
8. Glorification—Wild Dance [Amazons], after Herodotus [="*Glorification de l'Élue*"]
9. Action of the Elders [="*Action rituelle des Ancêtres*"]
10. Holy Dance [="*Danse sacrale*"]

Comparison of this list with the finished score discloses a few minor refinements to the scenario. Two merit comment. A little section was added before No. 9, entitled "Appeal to the

Forefathers". This was a reference to one of Roerich's most famous paintings, "Forefathers of Humankind", showing shamans in bearskins, which Roerich copied in designing the costumes for the ballet. The most significant change was the transfer of No. 5, the Game of Abduction, from its position right before the final dance in Part I to a position right after No. 1. It showed Stravinsky's readiness, when push came to shove, to sacrifice ethnological authenticity to artistic effect.

The Game of Abduction was the dance with which Stravinsky began composition in the summer of 1910, and it vividly illustrates his early commitment to ethnological authenticity. It is based on two folk songs, both of them avatars of the old Kupala rites. The first was a ceremonial dance-song *(khorovod)* from Rimsky-Korsakov's folk song anthology of 1877 (which Stravinsky had mined in both his previous ballets), with a text describing a game of snatching a bouquet (i.e. a bride), an atavism of precisely the action the music was to accompany in the ballet. The second, on which the middle section of the dance was fashioned, was an "Ivanovskaya"—a song sung on St. John's Eve (midsummer)—which Stravinsky, possibly prompted by Roerich, had found in a folksong anthology published by the Imperial Geographical Society. Its text, too, resonates exactly with the action: "Oh I'm running, running for a bride" *(Oy da ya bezhu, bezhu po pózhenke)*.

But then, having sketched this dance, Stravinsky became sidetracked with *Petrushka,* and did not hesitate to insert the piece into his new project—as the "Russian Dance" *(Russkaya)* performed by the puppets at the end of the First Tableau. In the new context, the carefully searched-out folk songs no longer bore the slightest relationship to the action. Again artistic expediency won out over scholarly propriety— but what of that? Stravinsky was an artist, not a scholar; his scholarly investigations were meant only to prime the creative pump. However fascinating to us eaves- droppers they were his business, not ours.

When he returned to *The Rite* in 1911, Stravinsky continued to prime his pump at the folkish fount. Themes for the Introduction, for dance 1,

for the newly-composed and newly-positioned Game of Abduction, and for the prefatory incantation preceding the Ceremonial Dance (Spring Rounds), were found in a vast collection of Lithuanian weddings songs edited by a Polish priest named Anton Juszkiewicz, which Stravinsky evidently consulted because (as Roerich may have told him) it was only among the Lithuanians and the Letts that animal sacrifices associated with Kupala were performed within living memory. The main theme of the Spring Rounds was a Semik song from the Rimsky-Korsakov collection. The theme of the Dance of the Earth at the end of Part I, the most orgiastic number in *The Rite,* can be identified with the genre of dance-until-you-drop ostinato variations most famously represented in Russian art music, as we have seen, by Glinka's *Kamarinskaya.* (The tune as first entered in the sketchbook bears a strong resemblance to a famous wedding song, "The dove flew cooing," or *Letal golub vorkoval.*) The main tune of the Ceremonial Dances at the beginning of Part II, was adapted from an ancient wedding song— appropriate enough for a dance through which Yarilo's bride was to be chosen. That of the Action of the Elders, right before the culminating sacrificial dance, was derived from a *vesnyanka,* an ancient charm that served in pagan times to "call in the spring."

Yet there was a great difference between Stravinsky's use of folklore and his teacher Rimsky-Korsakov's. Where the composers of Rimsky's or Balakirev's "nationalist" generation sought subject matter in folklore, and proudly displayed their borrowed artifacts, Stravinsky followed the practices of a later generation of artists known as "neonationalists," who sought in folkore not thematic content but stylistic renewal. Accordingly, Stravinsky subjected his borrowed melodies to extravagant transformations

that produced some of his most radical musical constructs. It is usually impossible to tell that a folk source is being employed in *The Rite* without studying the composer's sketches. (And no amount of study can tell us that we have identified all sources.) But the deeper the folk themes were submerged in the novel musical texture, the more they thus receded from view, the more pervasive and determinant their stylistic influence became.

Far from the purely intuitive, abstract music Stravinsky later claimed here to have written, there had never been a music more completely Russian in manner and attitude. And it was precisely what was most traditional about it that gave rise to the technical novelties (particularly in the rhythmic domain) that so captivated and influenced musicians in the West.

The same can be said of the ballet's harmonic idiom, adapted from the eight-tone scale Rimsky-Korsakov had derived from a study of Liszt. Again, however, though proceeding from established methods, Stravinsky made a maximalizing application that so accorded with notions of primitivistic immediacy (what in Russian is called *stikhíya*) that "cultured" musicians everywhere, even Debussy, took fright. The level of dissonance—produced by mixing octatonically-derived harmonies that earlier Russian composers had deployed in sequence—was so outlandishly high that, coupled with archaically modal melodies and radically simplified formal procedures (not to mention the crashing orchestration), the ballet sounded a note of irresistible violence and seeming rejection of all (European) tradition. ("Imagine!" wrote Vyacheslav Karatâgin, an early Russian reviewer, "from first note to last there is not a single common triad.") That is what made *The Rite of Spring* a modernist legend. But behind its revolutionary exterior lay an extraordinary synthesis of native folk and art traditions. These are what lent Stravinsky's masterpiece its phenomenal cultural authenticity, allowing it to outlive its legend and achieve its unshakeable status as a classic within the very tradition it had at first appeared to subvert.

BROOKLYN PHILHARMONIC ORCHESTRA

Dennis Russell Davies, Principal Conductor
Lukas Foss, Conductor Laureate
40th Season, 1993/94

Interplay: The Russian Stravinsky

Majestic Theater
May 8, 1 to 7 PM

DMITRI POKROVSKY, conductor

THE POKROVSKY ENSEMBLE
Members of the **BROOKLYN PHILHARMONIC ORCHESTRA**

1:00 — Introduction: Joseph Horowitz and Richard Taruskin

PART I: *Renard* (1915-16)

1:30 — Folk sources, including traditional travelling theater stories and songs

Skomorokh: Alexander Gordyenko, Sergei Zhirkov, Michael
Korzin, Dmitri Grishin, Tamara Smyslova, Elena Sergeyeva

2:00 — Renard

First Tenor: Sergei Zhirkov
Second Tenor: Dmitri Grishin
First Bass: Eygenny Vedernikov
Second Bass: Eygenny Tarasov

Members of the Brooklyn Philharmonic Orchestra

Intermission

PART II: *Stravinsky and Diaghilev's "World of Art"*

2:50 — a presentation with slides by John E. Bowlt

Intermission

PART III: *Les noces* (1921-23)

4:00 — Folk sources, including wedding ceremonies from southern and western Russia

Gusly: Sergei Zhirkov
Violinist: Michael Korzin

5:00 — Les noces

Part I: First Tableau: The Braid
Second Tableau: At the Groom's
Third Tableau: Seeing Off the Bride

Part II: Fourth Tableau: The Wedding Feast

Bride: Olga Uketcheva
Groom: Eygenny Vedernikov
Lament: Tamara Smyslova
Mother of the Bride: Tamara Smyslova
Mother of the Groom: Elena Sergeyeva
Drujki: Dmitri Grishin and Dmitri Fokin
Svashka: Maria Nefiodova
Skomoroshek: Alexander Prianikov

Timpani: Richard Fitz
Percussion: James Preiss, David Frost, William Trigg,
Charles Descarfino, Gordon Gottlieb

MX 100 Mark II Disklaviers provided by
Yamaha Corporation of America Keyboard Division

Intermission

5:50 — **PANEL DISCUSSION** with audience participation
John E. Bowlt, Dennis Russell Davies, Lukas Foss, Theodore Levin, Dmitri Pokrovsky,
Richard Taruskin, Elizabeth Kridl Valkenier
Joseph Horowitz, moderator

Support for these interpretive programs has been made possible by
**The Division of Public Programs, Public Humanities Projects of the
National Endowment for the Humanities.**

THE STANLEY H. KAPLAN EDUCATIONAL CENTER ACOUSTICAL SHELL
The Brooklyn Philharmonic and the Brooklyn Academy of Music gratefully acknowledge the generosity of
Mr. and Mrs. Stanley H. Kaplan, whose assistance made possible the Stanley H. Kaplan Educational Center Acoustical Shell.

SYNOPSES

RENARD

A Rooster, a Cat, and a Ram live happily together. One day, the Rooster is left to guard the house while the Ram and Cat are out. Along comes the Fox dressed as a nun. The Fox/nun convinces the Rooster that he has sinned with too many wives. The Rooster, ready to confess, gets trapped by the Fox. The Rooster cries for help. The Ram and the Cat come along just in time. The Fox runs off and all is calm.

Once more the Rooster is left to guard the house while the Ram and the Cat are away. The Fox appears dressed as a peasant woman. The Fox/peasant woman tells the Rooster she will give him beans. Unable to resist, the Rooster is trapped by the Fox. The Rooster cries in vain as the Fox begins to pluck his feathers. The Ram and Cat arrive.

A chase begins. The Ram and Cat, armed with a sickle, chase the Fox to his lair. The Ram and Cat sing the favorite songs of the Fox in an attempt to lure him from his lair. The Fox at the same time begins a conversation with himself. In this he discovers that his tail is a traitor trying to slow him down in the chase. Disgusted, the Fox gives his tail to the Ram and Cat to kill. Unfortunately for the Fox, all of his body is pulled from the lair and the Ram and Cat kill their enemy. The Rooster, Cat, and Ram rejoice.

LES NOCES

Part I:

First Tableau: "The Braid" (the bride's house, the morning of the wedding)

Les noces opens with the lament of the bride, a hysterical, haunting wailing. Surrounded by her maiden friends *(podruzhki)* and family, she is ritually prepared for the ceremony.   These are the bride's last hours in her house before her groom takes her away, perhaps forever. Her *podruzhki* offer consolation, praising her future husband and family. At the same time, the *svashenka* removes the red ribbon from the bride's hair—a symbol of virginity—and plaits her one braid into two. The mother of the bride calls to the Virgin Mary to help the *svakha*.   The Tableau closes with the bride crying for her scarlet ribbon and her friends repeating, almost mechanically, words of consolation. This mechanical frame provided by the *podruzhki* highlights the bride's hysteria.

Second Tableau: "At the Groom's"

A different mood permeates the house of the groom. The groom and his friends prepare for the wedding the way an army prepares for a dangerous battle. The groom's hair is combed and charmed to insure victory. He asks for his troops to be blessed as they prepare to seize the "capital city," i.e., the bride. The groom's father and guests bless the groom and his army with appeals to various Russian saints. The army, with the groom in the lead, begins the march.

Third Tableau: "Seeing Off the Bride" (house of the bride)

The bride and groom are blessed by their parents. Well-wishers accompany the betrothed as they leave for the church ceremony. The tableau ends with the two crying mothers, who, according to tradition, are not allowed to attend the actual wedding ceremony.

Part II:

Fourth Tableau: "The Wedding Feast" (house of the groom)

The guests are seated at a large table as the feast unravels. Scraps of conversation among the guests grow wilder and more provocative, and teasing refrains are sung to various guests. The mother of the bride officially gives her daughter to the groom. A specially chosen married couple warms the bed for the newlyweds. The curtain closes as the groom leads his wife to the bed and the guests sit quietly in front of the bedroom.

NB: Stravinsky marked *attaca subita* at the end of the first three tableaux, indicating no pauses between scenes.

With Renard *(1915-16) and* Les noces *(1921-23), we arrive at Stravinsky's densest folkloric style — works which fit no category, and which altogether elude adequate comprehension without recourse to rustic ritual. Richard Taruskin calls* Les noces *"perhaps the epitome of the neo-nationalist idea" of the poets and painters of* Mir isskustva *in its last phase — a period sometimes tagged "neo-primitivism."*

Stravinsky here created ensembles calculated to negate the lyricism and personal emotion associated with Western concert music. Les noces, *in particular, is intended to sound as mechanical as the interlocking fragments of song and speech comprising the score's machine-tooled wheels and cogs. Our performance, conducted by Dmitri Pokrovsky, accordingly uses mechanical pianos (see page 22).*

Renard is a "burlesque" for clowns, dancers, or acrobats. Stravinsky suggests that it be played on a trestle stage with the orchestra placed behind. The scoring is for flute, oboe, clarinet, bassoon, two horns, trumpet, percussion, timpani, cimbalom, solo string quintet, and four vocalists — two tenors and two basses. Le noces *is a set of "Russian choregraphic scenes" for four-part chorus with four soloists — soprano, mezzo, tenor, and bass. After exploring various alternatives, Stravinsky settled on an instrumental ensemble consisting of four pianos, xylophone, timpani, and percussion.*

The text for Renard *was adapted by Stravinsky from Alexander Afanasyev's collection of Russian folk tales. (For a synopsis, see page 50; the libretto may be found on page 58). The words for* Les noces *were adapted by Stravinsky from Russian popular texts collected by Pyotr Kireyevsky. (For a synopsis, see page 50, for the libretto, page 60).*

The first performance of Renard *took place at the Paris Opera on May 18, 1922. The company was the Ballets Russes, with decor and costumes by Mikhail Larionov and choreography by Bronislava Nijinska, who also danced the title role. The conductor was Ernest Ansermet. The first performance of* Les noces, *also by the Ballets Russes, took place at the Théâtre de la Gaieté Lyrique, Paris, with decor and costumes by Natalia Goncharova and choreography by Nijinska, Ansermet conducted.*

In the program notes that follow, Richard Taruskin takes issue with Dmitri Pokrovsky's contention (see page 21) that Renard *and* Les noces *integrate authentic Russian folk music; rather, Taruskin believes, Stravinsky is a "fabricator of authentic folklore." Taruskin's view of the "anti-humanist" implications of* Renard *and* Les noces *is also controversial (see pages 11and 23.)*

Notes on the Program

by Richard Taruskin

I t was after a performance of Stravinsky's *Baika pro Lisu, Petrushka, Kota da Barana* (Fable of the Vixen, the Cock, the Cat and the Ram, known in the West as *Renard*) that a Berlin critic wrote discerningly of the composer's anti-humanistic conception of "the folk" as a "collectively experiencing community related by clan—the primeval womb of all symbols and myths, the metaphysical forces of which religion is constructed." Nationalism, so characterized, was in 1948 impugned by the German sociologist Theodor W. Adorno for conveying an "affirmative ideology" (that is, one that upholds an unjust social order) which "re-appeared in Germany in a sinister context." Was this fair?

It seems a rather extravagant claim to make about a "merry performance with singing and music," which is how *Renard* is defined in its subtitle. In composing it, Stravinsky was attempting a sort of restoration— "a renaissance," as the critic Boris Asafyev put it, "of the art and trade of the *skomorokh* [the Russian minstrel player, the secularized descendent of the pre-Christian priestly caste], of the authentic 'old-time' Russian theater, a world of mockery, fun-and-games, tomfoolery, naughty satire— in sum, of a profoundly indigenous *grotesque.*"

Together with *Les noces, Renard* is the dazzling evocation of an ancient Russia that never was, but that in its intense artistic imagining was far "realer-than-the-real," as art alone could be. Its words are a brilliantly executed collage of no fewer than fifteen texts—narratives *(skazki),* ditties *(pesenki),* sayings *(poslovitsï),* and jingles *(pribautki)*—that Stravinsky found in Alexander Afanasyev's epochal collection of Russian folk tales, a multivolume compendium that came out in the middle of the nineteenth century, and quickly took its place in Russia alongside its prototype by the brothers Grimm, published in Germany a generation before. As a genre, the acted-out folktale was Stravinsky's own invention, but it

has an uncanny ring of ethnic authenticity, since it bridges two genres—orally disseminated stories and *skomorosh'ye deystvo* (minstrel play)—whose close relationship historians have long assumed but have never been able to prove. Stravinsky, not a historian preserving his source material but an artist commandeering it, fearlessly forged the missing link, and did it with magnificent aplomb, mastering the diction of Asafyev's peasant informants as if it were his native speech.

The music, as in *Les noces,* is a collage—phrases, refrains, little tunes—in which not a single one is merely quoted. All are created. No Russian composer before or since equalled Stravinsky as the fabricator of authentic folklore. He dreamed up an imaginary ethnic culture and painstakingly transcribed its folk music. Then he called it "Russia." He scored the music thus obtained for an ensemble that, like one of the preliminary *Les noces* ensembles, featured the Hungarian cimbalom. Stravinsky first encountered this instrument in 1915 in a Geneva restaurant, played by a Hungarian virtuoso named Aladar Racz, who gave the composer some lessons on it and received from him some little pieces and arrangements he continued to perform until his death in 1956. Stravinsky immediately recognized in the dulcimer-like cimbalom a serviceable substitute for the Russian gusli, a psaltery-like folk instrument known to have been used by the Russian minstrels. It is altogether possible that the whole idea for composing *Renard* came to Stravinsky when he discovered the little jingle in Afanasyev in which an old man who owns a pretty little cock entertains it by playing his gusli: *Stren'-bren', moi gusel'tsï, / Zolotãye moi strunochki!* (Strum, strum, my little gusli, my little golden strings). An adaptation of these lines, comically given to the ram (whose hooved forelegs could hardly have strummed a gusli) introduces the final episode in the play, culminating in the vixen's violent demise.

According to Robert Craft, Stravinsky wished to have *Renard* performed in the language of its audience, whatever that might be. And yet, as the composer put it himself, "the music of *Renard* begins in the verse." So dependent is the rhythmic structure of the music on the forceful accentual patterns of the Russian language—patterns honored both in the observance and, just as purposefully and meaningfully, in the breach—that translations of *Renard* always sing clumsily, playing the incredible deftness of the setting utterly false. Besides, hardly anything is lost when the words are not immediately understood. As Charles-Ferdinand Ramuz, the Swiss poet and novelist who translated *the Baika* into French as *"Renard"*, said of his original text for Stravinsky's *Soldier's Tale* (also based, albeit loosely, on Afanasyev), "this is not a play, it is a story." *Renard* may not even be a story. It is a sublime mishmash in which the story as such is intelligible in a staged performance only on the visual plane. The text, hovering perpetually—even (or especially) in the original—on the brink of nonsense, dispenses with linear narrative altogether. The plot is interrupted for unannounced and unidentified digressions, interpolations and flashbacks, and the charac

Broadside showing a tale of the Fox and the Cock, as in *Renard* (Moscow, 1852).

ters—impersonated now by one voice, now by another, now by voices in tandem or tutti—are fragmented and absorbed into the musical texture to the point where in a concert performance there is no hope of following the plot in any but the most general terms, and then

only if one has read a synopsis. (Here it is, in one sentence: A vixen twice seduces a cock to come down from his perch into her clutches and is first chased away, then slain, by the tomcat and the ram.) The music, though it arose from the words, no longer follows them but leads. Asafyev's shrewd comment about *Soldier's Tale,* Stravinsky's other minstrel show, applies with even greater justice to *Renard*:

> Despite the syncretic plan it is chiefly a musical composition. Such is the fate of all attempts at artistic synthesis in the presence of music, itself the art of movement and transformation of the energy of sound: music immediately begins to dominate.

It does so, anyhow, if the composer is Stravinsky. Despite the fact that it is a sung piece while *Soldier's Tale* is a melodrama in which the actors speak and the music is wholly instrumental, the music of *Renard* is every bit as "absolute." To an extent unprecedented and never again equalled even by Stravinsky, he succeeded in making the words of his "merry performance" literally and indispensably *a part of the music.*

That music is an epitome—perhaps *the* epitome—of the neonationalist ideal that motivated the poets and painters of Russia in the decades preceding the revolution. No other artist ever managed to found a stylistic revolution so thoroughly on abstracted elements of folklore, both observed and invented. And that is precisely what made Stravinsky's work, even at its most

delightful and accessible (or rather, *precisely* at its most delightful and accessible), so sinister in Adorno's eyes. The German critic saw more clearly than any other at the time the way in which Stravinsky's neoprimitivist music was participating in a general stripdown from *kul'tura* to *stikhiya* (to put it in Russian terms), from humanistic "culture" to an "instinctual immediacy" that could easily devolve into mere biologism, the idea that life is no more than an unthinking, unfeeling instinct for survival. Stravinsky's musical innovations, amounting to a radical simplification of means, replaced the complexities of linear thought and reflective subjectivity with gnostic revelation and kinaesthetic response.

Where Stravinsky's enthusiasts saw his achievement as a miraculous *uproshcheniye,* as the Russians say, a "second simplicity" that brought thought and feeling to a higher synthesis, Adorno saw only what the Russians call an *oproshcheniye,* a dehumanizing retreat from intellectual engagement and an impoverishment of spirit. It is a controversy that has never entirely gone away. It threatens to burgeon anew as we become increasingly aware — far more aware than Adorno could have been — of Stravinsky's susceptibility to the allure of the sinister ideology of affirmation (let me say it straight out: the ideology of Mussolini and of Hitler) in the decades leading up to the Second World War.

* * *

> Every form of art has its starting point in reality, and its finishing point in music.
> —Andrey Belïy, *Symbolism* (1910)

. . . For two weeks or so
a woman matchmaker kept visiting
my kinsfolk, and at last
my father blessed me. Bitterly
I cried for fear; and, lamenting, they unbraided
my tress and, chanting, they led me to the
      church.
And so I entered a strange family.
      —Alexander Pushkin, *Eugene Onegin*
      (1833), Chapter Three, canto XVIII,
      lines 11-14 (trans. Vladimir Nabokov)

Two rivers have flowed together,
Two matchmakers have come together,
They thought a thought about a blond tress:
"How shall we unbraid this tress?
How shall we divide the braid in two?"
      —*Songs Collected by P. V. Kireyevsky.*
      New Series, volume I (Moscow, 1911),
      no. 999

Fair maids, cooking whizzes, pot smashers,
proud matrons, thin old grannies, puny
brats, zany rogues and piddling scoundrels:
SING YOUR SONGS!
      —*Songs Collected by P. V. Kireyevsky,*
      no. 806 (trans. William Harkins):
      Svadebka, Tableau IV, fig. 112

The first thought of a scenic representation of the *svadebnïy obryad,* the elaborate Russian peasant wedding ritual, came to Igor Stravinsky in 1912, while he was composing the second tableau of *The Rite of Spring,* his "icy comedy of primeval hysteria" (in the words of Andrey Levinson, its most perceptive reviewer). The first performance of *Svadebka,* subtitled "Russian choreographic scenes with singing and [instrumental] music," took place in Paris (under the title "Les noces villageoises") more than a decade later, on June 13, 1923. No other work would ever occupy Stravinsky even half as long. No other work would ever be as important to him. In *Les noces* — as we now call it in the West — Stravinsky reinvented in his imagination the Russia that had, over the course of the ballet's gestation, been lost to him in reality.

It was another icy comedy—an elegantly detached, non-narrative collage presentation of a ritual action that ends, like its predecessor, in a

scene of virgin sacrifice. The difference was that it was drawn from an exceedingly well-documented living tradition (or at the very least from customs that survived in living memory) rather than from a quasi-mythical archaic lore. It sought validation in ethnological fact (Belïy's "starting point in reality," as in the epigraphs above), but like *The Rite,* it refused to be bound by any limits such validation might imply. Its reality, like that of *The Rite,* was ultimately one created, not received. But it was a *Rite* in black and white—the literal black and white of four keyboards, plus percussion.

Finding this scoring was what took Stravinsky all that time. It superseded many preliminary versions that had tried in one way or another to reproduce the actual sounds of Russian folk instruments—one of them combined a pianola, a harmonium and two Hungarian cimbaloms—and gave the composer what he called the "perfectly homogeneous, perfectly impersonal, and perfectly mechanical" medium by which he could do justice to the depiction of a sacrament enacted with the "profound gravity and cool inevitable intention" that, in the words of a contemporary folklorist, befit any artifact of "remorseless, inelastic tradition." Despite its considerable clangor, not to mention the rowdy doings in its fourth tableau, *Les noces* makes an impression quite unlike the terrifying *Rite.* Where the earlier "pagan" ballet was orgiastic and "biological," *Les noces* is a work of dignity and reserve, finally of religious exaltation (specifically Christian, Stravinsky insisted). At a time of upheaval and ruin it offered a restorative view of the only eternity humans can know—the eternity of customs. At a time of existential trauma it offered the solacing prospect of life as liturgy.

What *The Rite* and *Les noces* have fundamentally in common is Stravinsky's lifelong anti-humanism—his rejection of all "psychology." The sacrificial virgin in *The Rite* does her fatal dance with animal fearlessness and the community accepts her ceremonial murder without compunction. The horrible denouement is presented

Natalia Goncharova,
Group of four dancers in *Les noces*
(1923).

as anything but horrible— and that's what's horrible. In *Les noces,* the bride laments at the outset and the groom leers in conclusion (to a variant of the same melody!) not because spontaneous feeling so prompts them, but because the immemorial script so decrees. There was of course a dark side to this celebration of the unthinking subjection of human personality to a implacably demanding—and, by Enlightened standards, an unjust—social order; and it came out into the open in the awful decades of economic disaster and nationalistic totalitarianism in

Plaiting ceremony, photographed in Karelia (1971).

the wake of the First World War. (Could something similar be brewing now, in the wake of the Cold War?) Whether it irrevocably taints Stravinsky and his work, as Adorno insisted, is something for us individually to decide in keeping with our own liberal traditions. The tension between nostalgia for the security of community and the obligations of enlightened individualism lives not only in *Les noces,* but also in ourselves as, contemplating it, we are emotionally swayed by its potent advocacy of what may appear on rational reflection to be a parlous message.

That thrilling if finally disquieting potency arises out of Stravinsky's miraculously successful transcendence of the particular. The musical and textual content of *Les noces* underwent a process of streamlining and abstraction as stringent as

that to which the scoring was subjected. Originally the composer planned a detailed narrative scenario in three acts, constructed out of the work of the Romantic- nationalist ("Slavophile") Russian ethnographers of Pushkin's time, the early nineteenth century— Ivan Sakharov, Vasiliy Tereshchenko, Pyotr Kireyevsky. Act I was to have depicted the *Smotreniye,* the Bride Show, at which the groom's matchmaker inspects the prospective bride and strikes a bargain by a literal striking of hands *(rukobit'ye)* with the bride's father. The second act was to have had three scenes. The first, in two parts, was to depict the bride's lament and the groom's ritual of exorcism; the second, also in two parts, was to show the hair-plaiting ceremony at the bridal shower *(devichnik)* and the preparations for the ritual bath of purification; the third would take place at the bride's house right before the departure for church. Act III would have shown the wedding feast itself.

In the end, seizing on Kireyevsky's song no. 999 (given as an epigraph above), which he adopted for a while as the metaphorical epigraph to his score, Stravinsky rejected narrative in favor of what the formalist anthropologists of his day called a "morphological" (and what we today, following a related anti-humanistic discourse, would call a "structuralist") reading of the Russian folk tradition. Elements from the peasant rite were freely extracted and juxtaposed to create a vivid artistic shape in two great metaphorical waves. Tableaus I and II, centering on the bride's and the groom's coiffures, depict the "rivers," Tableau III (the old Act II, sc. iii) would show their confluence: that is the first wave. Tableau IV (the old Act III), as long as all the rest combined, depicts the wedding feast *(krasnïy stol,* literally the "beautiful table") and aims with mounting excitement at the procreative consummation, for the sake of which the rite exists. The progressive insinuation of the opening melody from the first tableau

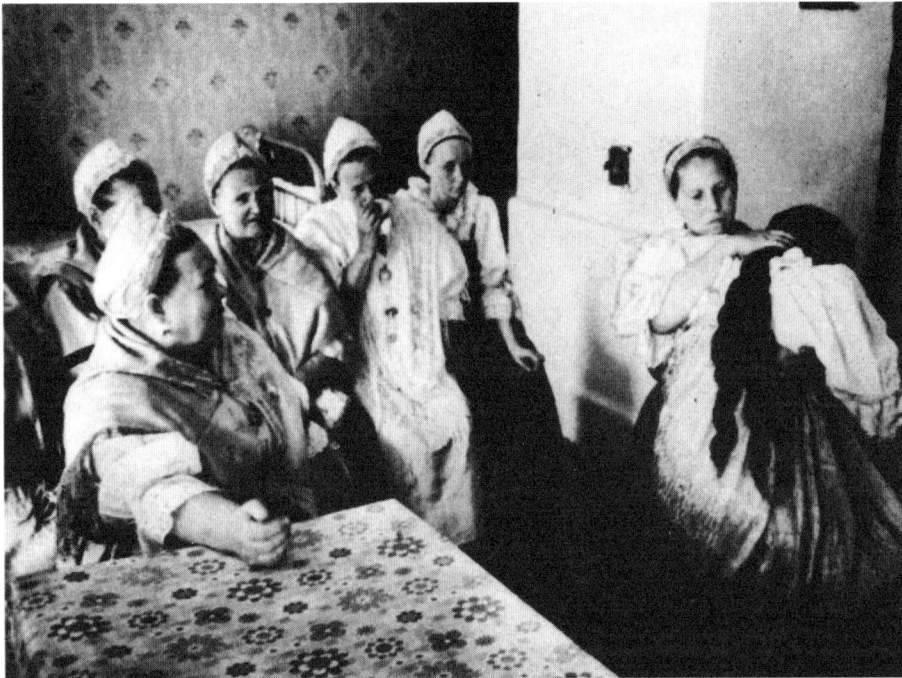

into the concluding pages of the fourth adds a new metaphorical level, and the imitation of bells proclaiming eternity to the same strains at the very end caps the point.

Stravinsky's music abstracts three styles of peasant singing. Lament *(plach)* and chant *(peniye)*, as contrasted by Pushkin in the passage from *Eugene Onegin* quoted above as epigraph, provide the material for the first wave. (Stravinsky copied exactly the description of the Russian lamenting style—a three-note formula, sung with wailing timbre and vocalized breathing, and decorated with yodels— that he found in Vladimir Dahl's dictionary of the "living Great-Russian language," a monument of romantic nationalistic scholarship.) Songs *(pesni)*, as in the wedding-jester's exhortation in the final epigraph, form the substance of the second.

The unportrayed church ceremony forms the watershed that divides the waves; a suggestion of its music comes in the middle of the second tableau, with a duet for two basses accompanied by the female chorus that is modelled on an authentic church chant, and that was first sketched in 1914 for a projected ballet called *Liturgiya.* Except for the melody that brings the fourth tableau to its culmination, a lyrical folk song Stravinsky that took down from the singing of his friend Stepan Mitusov (the sheet on which he notated it—with difficulty!—survives in his Archive), the remaining tunes in *Les noces* are of ethnographically authentic, identifiable cast, but of Stravinsky's own invention. By the time he wrote *Les noces* Stravinsky could more easily make up a genuine Russian folk tune than look it up.

The composer organized his grand folklike mosaic of diatonic tunes around a harmonic structure derived, like that of *The Rite,* from the eight-note ("octatonic") scale of alternating tones and semitones, which had been pioneered by his teacher Rimsky-Korsakov. The hidden octatonic background that harmonizes and controls the audible diatonic surface is a perfect metaphor for the constraints of immemorial custom that invisibly rule the day-to-day currents of life in Stravinsky's imagined folk world, harmonizing the thoughts and actions of individuals with the transcendent organic community of the

composer's dreams, lending his ballet both its incomparable aesthetic integrity and its ominously alluring political appeal.

To perform the work, as is being done at BAM, with vocal parts sung in authentic ethnic style by the Pokrovsky Ensemble, at once points up Stravinsky's ethnographic accuracy and (by, as it were, "de-universalizing" the piece and rendering it the more exotic) somewhat moderates and marginalizes its political message. It suggests the way Stravinsky might have conceived the work before the revolution, when he thought of himself as a Europeanized Russian writing for other Europeanized Russians in aestheticized celebration of the ur-Russian. His implied call, after the revolution, to Russianize and orthodoxly Christianize the world, in response to Russia's capitulation to the atheistic, positivistic, "European" heresy of Marxism, is muted.

It was a call that his fellow émigrés, especially that violently anti-European faction known as the "Eurasianists," heard clearly and did their best to publicize, hailing Stravinsky as a kind of musical Messiah, at war with a flabbily liberal, debilitated West. (The leader, or at least the bankroller, of the Eurasianists was Pyotr Suvchinsky, the heir to a tea fortune, who from the 1920s to the composer's death was one of Stravinsky's closest confidants.) Even after he turned "cosmopolitan," Stravinsky's art continued its propaganda against the modern world of politics. His "neoclassical" art continued its propaganda for a vicarious imperial and orthodox restoration. That propaganda can be read with particular clarity in his Harvard lectures of 1939, published as *Poetics of Music,* for which Suvchinsky had been among the ghostwriters.

RENARD

A Burlesque for Singing and Acting

MARCH *(to accompany the entrance of the players)*
(The Cock is fidgeting on his perch).
Tenor I: Chuck-chuck-chuck-chuck-chuck-chuck-a-dah. Chuck-a-dah.
Bass I: I'm the king of my yard. Chuck-a-dah.
Tenor I: Knock his ribs in for him.
Tenor II: With our spurs gore him.
Bass II: Beat him, beat him black and blue, then stick a knife into him.
Tenor I: Chuck-chuck-chuck-chuck-chuck-chuck-a-dah. Chuck-a-dah.
Bass I: Bring him to me quickly. Chuck-a-dah.
Bass II: Come on, don't wait, you'll be too late. Chuck-a-dah.
Bass I: Chuck-chuck-chuck-chuck-chuck-chuck-chuck-chuck-chuck-chucka-dah. Chuck-a-dah.
Bass II: Chuck-a-dah.
Tenor I & Bass I: Now the knife is ready.
Tenor I & II: It's a very sharp knife.
Bass I & II: Say good-bye to your life. He'll get such a banging, then there'll be a hanging.
Tenor I: Chuck-chuck-chuck-chuck-chuck-chuck-a-dah. Chuck-a-dah.
Bass I: For the knife is ready waiting, and the rope is oscillating. He'll get such a banging, banging followed by a hanging, hanging.
Tenor I: This barnyard is my throne — my hens are all my own — I crow alone.
(Enter Renard dressed as a nun)
Tenor II: Greetings, my little redhead beauty. Put aside your pride and come down sir. Tell me all your sins. I come from deserts far away, nothing to eat today.
(The Cock, impatiently)
Tenor I: Get along old fox.
(Renard, continuing)
Tenor II: I can't tell you what I've suffered. But now, dearest boy, I shall give you absolution.
(The Cock, arrogantly)
Tenor I: Oh, my good old Brother Renard. Chuck-a-dah. Now I have to be on my guard. Chuck-a-dah. When you come to my yard. Chuck-a-dah.
Tenor II: Oh, my son, listen to me. Though you sit up high you're a sinner. I'll tell you why, so take heed, my son. Hear what you've done. All your kind have too many wives. Some have ten wives or more. Other a score. Twenty wives are cause for much trouble. How much more if their numbers double. You are always fighting, squabbling over all

your wives as if they were your sweethearts. Come, approach son, I'll hear your confession.
Tenor I & II: So that you be spared the risk of dying in sin.
(The Cock prepares to jump - "salto mortale.")
(He jumps)
(Renard seizes the Cock and goes round the stage holding him under his arm.)
(The Cock struggles desperately.)
Tenor I: Help, oh help, oh help, oh help! He's got me by the tail, he's pulled me off my rail — torn me all to bits — won't let me go. Oh — oh! Dragging me miles away, how many miles I can't say, ten, twenty or more, surely more than a score I should say! Br'er cat — don't let him devour me. Save me, my friends, or he'll overpower me. I'm so afraid. Oh-oh-come to my aid!
(Enter the Cat and the Goat)
Bass I: Ha, ha, ha, my good fellow Renard. What you've got there shows us you've been robbing the barnyard.
Bass I & II: Don't you want to part with it? You know we're honest men, and will pay our share, and play fair.
Tenor I: So drop it, or you will feel the stick.
(Renard lets the Cock go and runs away. The Cat and the Goat dance.)
Bass I: Ho, Renard, we can lick you. Ho, in jail we'll quickly stick you.
Bass I & II: Boasting what he had done and what he would do, it's true. He'd a thing to smash every bone in your body so he boasted.
Tenor II: Now we see the Cock out walking.
Bass I & Tenor II: Out walking. With him go all his lady wives.
Bass I & II: Lady wives.
Tenor II: All his little dear chickens.
Bass I: Lucky-lucky.
Bass II: One by one he now can count them. One by one he now will mount them.
Bass I & II: Not far off is Brother Renard - he gives warning.
Bass I: "Have a care, my dear; you're done, I fear. You'll catch it now, my dear fine fellow."
Tenor II: Please don't eat me, Brother Fox.
Bass I: Please don't eat me, Brother Fox. Take my wife but don't take me...
Tenor I: It's your corpse I must have alone. Skin and bones, all skin and bones!
Tenor I & II; Bass I & II: Oh-oh-oh-oh-oh
Bass I & II: So the sly old...
Bass I:...Renard came and hooked him.
Bass I & II: From the wall...
Bass I: ...he jumped and tooked him. By

the neck he grabbed him. With his sharp teeth he nabbed him.
Bass II: Chuck-chuck-chuck-chuck-a-chuck-chuck-chuck-chuck.
(The Cat and the Goat retire)
Bass I & II: But the hens don't hear, they're dreaming.
(The Cock climbs onto his perch again and settle down comfortable.)
Tenor I: This barnyard is my throne. My hens are all my own. I crow alone.
(Enter Renard. He throws off his nun's disguise.)
Tenor II: Chuck-a-chuck, good master. Cock with your fine scarlet crest, dressed in your best, looking so bold in your coat of gold, so now open the door, pray.
Tenor I: No, I will not open.
Tenor II: I'll give you some green peas.
Tenor I: No peas for me, I've spoken.
Tenor I: The only thing we cocks like is grain, you talk in vain.
Bass I: Cocky, Cocky, dear Cock. I've a house quite full of lovely ripe grain. You shall have as much as you could ever eat-eat-eat.
Bass I: What?
Bass I - Tenor I: No, I can't.
Tenor II: Chuck-a-chuck, good master Cock, with your fine scarlet crest, dressed in your best, looking so bold in your coat of gold. I've brought you some breadcrumbs.
Tenor I: You bore me with your breadcrumbs. You're a fool, yes, a fool. I'll mind my business, you mind yours.
Bass I: Cocky, dear Cocky, dear Cock.
Bass I & II:...Come down from where you perch so high, my boy.
Bass I: Why are you afraid to come...
Bass I & II: ...to me. You must see that I'm as friendly as can be.
(The Cock prepares to jump — "salto mortale")
Tenor I: *(shouting)* Don't eat me, Renard. I'm too fat!
(The Cock jumps. Renard seizes him.)
Tenor II: Some like it fat and some like it lean!
(Renard goes around the stage holding the Cock under his arm, who is struggling desperately).
Tenor I: Help, oh help, oh help, oh help. He's got hold of my crest, he's clawing at my breast. He's got hold of my tail. Naked I shall be like a little Jesus, nothing left only skin. Come help me; I'm in danger, my God. Who would believe this could happen?
Br'er Goat, Br'er Cat, Oh, why don't you come to me? Br'er Goat, Br'er Cat, how can you do this to me? Br'er Goat, Br'er Cat!
Tenor I & II: He will tear me to bits.
(Renard carries off the Cock to the side of the stage and begins to pull out his feathers. The Cock begs for mercy.)
Tenor I: Ah, Renard, Brother Renard, be kind to me, have pity on me, as my guest come

home with me and see how happy you will be and you will see how lovely a life we lead. How we feed a richer spread — butter upon the bread. Master take care of me, my cousin Maxar, Godmother Zaxar and the Saints, my Patron Pyetrom, Uncle Mirayed, Granny Blyematcka and dear Aunt Katyusha, Grandmother Matrushu.
(The Cock passes out.)
(Enter the Cat and the Goat. Accompanying themselves on the "guzla" they sing for Renard a nice little song.)
Bass I: Plinc, plinc. We'll sing you a pretty song, not too long. Plinc, plinc.
Bass I & II: A pretty song we'll sing you. Plinc, plinc. All for the love of you. It's not long but it's something quite new.
Bass I: Plinc, plinc. We'll sing you a pretty song, not too long. Plinc, plinc.
Bass II: Are you there, old Brother Fox?
Bass I: Are you there, old Brother Fox?
Bass II: Are you there, old Brother Fox?
Bass I: I don't see you, Brother Renard, where are you? Plinc, plinc.
Bass II: Is he there? Is he there? I want...
Bass I & II: ...to see him, speak to him and to his sweet daughters.
Bass I: Plinc, plinc. We'll sing you a pretty song, not too long. Plinc, plinc.
Bass II: The first daughter's called Sleek-and-Sly.
Bass I & II: The second daughter's called Smooth-as-Silk.
Bass I: Number three Butter-Belly.
Bass II: And number four is Cinnamon-Browny.
Bass I: Plinc, plinc. We'll sing you a pretty song, not too long. Plinc, plinc.
Bass I & II: A pretty song we'll sing you. Plinc, plinc. All for love of you, it's not long, but it's something quite new. Are you there, old Brother Fox? What are you doing now? Where are you Brother Fox? I don't see you. Brother Renard, where are you?
(Renard pokes his nose out.)
Tenor II: Who is making this row? Who is there, what do you want now?
Bass I & II: What will happen now you'll see. But it won't happened to me. In our hands a great big knife. We've come to take your life.
(The animals brandish a big knife. Renard is terrified.)
Tenor I: Oh my eyes, oh you precious pair of eyes, what have you done now, what have you been doing?
Bass I & II: Watching over you, always to save you from all your wicked foes.
Tenor I: Oh, you, my feet, so fleet in your running, how have you helped me with all your great cunning?

Bass I & II: Well, we ran away so fast from your pursuers you escaped at last.
Tenor I: My tail you've brought me bad luck.
Tenor II & Bass II: In the hedge I got stuck.
Bass I: Wasn't that just rotten luck?
Tenor I & II; Bass I & II: Thus I helped them all to trap you,
Bass I & II: ...that they might snap you.
(Renard, in a rage, lashes his tail. Addressing it, he cries...)
Tenor I: You scoundrel, let the beasts tear you to bits.
(The animals catch Renard by the tail, pull him out of his house and strangle him. The two Tenors and the two Basses shout at the top of their voices. Renard expires. The Cock, the Cat and the Goat begin to dance.)
Bass I: Brother Fox, dear Foxy, why do you now desert me?
Tenor II: 'Cos I've work to do at home.
Tenor I: I must do it all alone.
Bass I: Your wife has been misled, sir.
Tenor I: Someone's in your bed, sir, and the hounds are baying.
Tenor II: And their pups are playing.
Bass I & II; Tenor I: They are telling Renard —
Bass I: Eh, Renard, why do you wait? Foxy might be too late!
Tenor I: Foxy might be too late!
Tenor II; Bass II: Foxy!
Bass I: Renard says, "Is that so?" Have some drink and let's go. All about the village wolves are trampling tillage. Renard still is shirking, 'neath the stove he's lurking. He's leaping to the ground, emitting a loud sound.
Tenor I & II: Patazoum! So much better for the hens.
Bass I: Soon all cares will mend.
Tenor I & II: Zoum! zoum! zoum! patazoum!
Bass I: Here's the story's end.
Tenor I & II: Zoum! zoum! zoum! patazoum! patazoum! patazoum! patazoum!
Tenor II: We are leaving right away -
Tenor I: We have not eaten today.
Tenor II: Five, one, two, one, two, one -
Tenor I: - two, one, two, three, four...
Tenor I & II: ...five, one, two, one, two, one, two...
Tenor I & II: ...one, two, three, four, five...
Bass I; Tenor I & II: ...one, two, one, two, one.
Bass I: If our play's not funny, pray, put the blame on Johnny. John Barley Corn, just this and nothing more.
Tenor I & II: He's just a scarecrow.
Bass I: Burn him at the hedgerow.
Bass I: In honor of you all...
Tenor I & II: ...our masters came with their hounds.
Bass I & II: On leash they're lying.
Bass I & II: The hounds were not contented.

For Renard they have scented.
Bass II: Now the story is done.
Tenor I: You must pay for your fun.
MARCH *(played while the actors make their exit)*
Now Renard's life is done.
(Spoken): And if my story's pleased you, please don't forget my fee's due.

LES NOCES

First Tableau

Bride:
My braid, my light-brown braid!
Last night, my mother plaited you, my braid,
My mother curled you in a silver ring.
The ruthless *svashenka* came, ruthless and
merciless! She began to tear and pinch the
braid.
And tearing and pinching, to braid it in two
(braids).

Podruzhki:
I'm combing and combing Nastasia's braid,
I'm combing and combing Timofeyevna's
light brown hair,
And again I'll comb it, and I'll plait it in a
braid,
With a scarlet ribbon I'll braid it.
I'm combing and combing Nastasia's braid,
I'm combing and combing Timofeyevna's
light brown hair,
I'm combing and combing, I'm combing the
light brown braid,
I'll part it with a fine-toothed comb.
I'm combing and combing Nastasia's braid,
I'm combing and combing Timofeyevna's
light brown hair,
And again I'll comb it and I'll plait it in a
braid,
I'll braid it with a scarlet ribbon, and weave it
together with a blue one.

Don't honk, don't honk, swan,
Don't honk in the field, white swan.
Don't cry, don't grieve, Nastasyushka,
Don't cry, don't be sad, dear Timofeyevna,
For father, for mother,
For the loud nightingale in the garden.
As a father-in-law, father
Will be kind to you,
As a mother-in-law, mother
Will be kind to you,
Will be sympathetic with you.

Khvetis, sir Pamfilevich
Is your nightingale in the garden,
In the high tower,
In the high, lavishly painted (tower).
During the day he whistles
And all night he sings.
You, you, Nastasyushka,
You, fair one, Timofeyevna,
He amuses, comforts,
Sleep long, he won't disturb you,
He'll wake you for afternoon mass.

Play, play, bold *skomoroshek*,
From village to village.
Paradise, paradise, that our Nastasyushka
Should be happy.

From under the stone, from under the white
stone a stream rushes.
From under the stone, from under the white
stone they're striking cimbaloms.
And they drink and they pour, and strike
cymbals.
Well, it seems that Nastyushka,
It seems that they're taking our Timofeyevna
to the wedding.

Mother of the Bride:
Holy Mother,
Come to our house
To help the *svakh* plait the braid,
Nastasyushka's braid,
Timofeyevna's light brown hair.

Bride:
Plait my light brown braid,
Oh, braid it tightly at the root,
Finely in the middle,
Put a little red ribbon at the end.
Oh, you, my ribbon, little red ribbon.
A scarlet ribbon, a flower bouqet ribbon
A violet ribbon.

Second Tableau: "At the Groom's"

Wedding Party of the Groom:
Holy Mother,
Come to our house
To help the *svakha*
To comb the curls,
Khvetis's curls,
To comb the curls,
Pamfilich's curls.
Come, come to our house.
With what should I comb, with what should
I oil Khvetis's curls?
With what should I comb, with what should
I oil Pamfilich's light brown hair?
We'll rush, we'll dash
to three market cities.
We'll buy, we'll buy
Oil from Provence.
We'll comb, we'll oil
Khvetis's curls.
We'll comb, we'll oil
Pamfilich's light brown hair.

Parents of the Groom Alternate:
Last night,
Khvetis sat in the tower,
Pamfilich sat,
Combing the light brown curls.
You, curls, to whom will you belong?
You, light brown hair, to whom will you
belong?
Curls, you'll belong to a beautiful girl.
That Nastasya Timofeyevna.
You, Nastasyushka, cherish those curls!

You, Timofeyevna, cherish the light-brown
hair.

Kvas, like raspberries, that ten people
poured.

Khvetis's curls curled and curled.
Pamfilich's light brown hair curled and curled.
Mother curled them,
She curled them and repeated:
"My child, be ruddy fresh
Ruddy fresh and safe from the evil eye."

He was whacked with a snowball tree branch
And washed with raspberries.

Whose curls, whose light-brown hair?
Khvetis's light-brown curls,
Pamfilich's combed,
Combed, oiled.

Glory, glory, to father and mother,
They bore a good child.
Smart and reasonable,
Obedient and well-spoken.

Nastasyushka, get used
To my clear face,
To my way of thinking,
To my dashing ways.

Be close, brown curls,
To my clear face,
To my way of thinking,
To my dashing ways.

And in Moscow, in Moscow,
People marveled at those curls.

Holy Mother,
Come to our house,
To help the *svakha*,
To comb the curls,
Khvetis's curls,
To comb the curls,
Pamfilich's curls.
Come, come to our house,
To comb the curls.
And you, Mother of God,
The Virgin Mary yourself,
Come to the wedding.
With all the Apostles
Come to the wedding.
With all the angels
Come to the wedding.
Bless, Lord, Bless Lord, Lord,
Come to the wedding, come to the wedding,
come to the wedding!

Groom:
Bless, father and mother,
Your child, to assault the capital city,

To bang a stone wall.
To know his intended,
To go to the cathedral, the church,
To kiss the silver cross.

Where Khvetis, sir, is sitting,
There, the Virgin will find candles.
God's grace, Virgin!

First Druzhko:
Onlookers, idlers,
Gapers and squabblers,
Everyone bless the newlywed prince
To go on his way,
To take the intended, the appointed
To stand under the golden crown!

The swan feather fell,
Ivan Paolo,
Fell down in front of the tower,
Ivan fell!
Khvetis fell down before his own father,
Pamfilich fell down before his own mother.
He asks: Bless me
To go to God's judgment,
To the holy coronation.
As God led under the cross
So let me be under the crown.

Bless, everyone, from old to young!
To play Cosmas and Demian
And so to play a wedding.
Bless, Lord the two who were born,
Bless, Lord the two who were born,
Bless the Lord, the two who are seated,
Bless, Lord, fellow traveler Mikita,
Archangel Michael.
Bless, Lord, the birth of Christ,
Bless, Lord, the Baptism,
To send to the crown
Bless, Lord, Lord,
Come to the wedding!

Saint Luke, come to the wedding,
Saint Luke, consummate the wedding,
Consummate the wedding of the two young
ones,
Consummate the wedding of the two seated
ones,
Consummate the wedding of the two
intended ones,
And the first born!

Third Tableau: "Seeing Off the Bride"

The bright moon was blessed
By the shining sun.
The princess was blessed
By the father, sir,
By the mother, ma'am.
Bless me, father,
To go to a foreign land.

Parents of the Bride:
The solid wax candle melted,
Standing long before the icon.
The princess stiffened her quick legs,
Crying bitterly before the father.

Druzhki:
Oh how they blessed the virgin,
Oh how they blessed her for good,
With bread and salt, with the icon of the Saviour.

Saint Cosmas, come to the wedding.
Saint Cosmas, Demian, come to the wedding.
Saint Cosmas, come to the wedding.
Saint Cosmas, forge us a wedding.
Saint Cosmas, forge us a strong one,
Strong, hard, long-lasting,
From youth to old age,
And to the little children.

In the room, in the front room,
Two doves on the beams.
They drink, they drink and pour,
They bang on a timpani,
They play along on cimbaloms.

Mother of Cosmas Demian
Walked about the porch
Collecting nails.

Saint Cosmas, come to the wedding,
Saint Cosmas, consummate the wedding.
From youth to old age,
 And to the little children.

Cosmas and Demian
Walked about the porch
Collecting nails
To forge a wedding.

And you, yourself, Mother of God,
You Mother of God, the Virgin yourself,
come to the wedding, consummate the wedding.
Consummate the wedding, consummate it strong.
With all the angels,
With all the Apostles.

As the hops curl around the stakes,
That's how our young ones
Would curl around each other.

Two Mothers:
My darling child,
Don't leave me, sorrowful,
Come back, come back, my child,
Come back, my darling.

My darling child,
I fed you and gave you drink.
Come back, my dear.
My child, you left
A bunch of golden keys

On a silk sash,
My darling child.

Fourth Tableau: The Wedding Feast

A berry rolled to a berry,
A berry bowed to a berry.

A berry is red.
The strawberry is ripe, ripe.

A berry bowed to a berry,
A berry said a word to a berry,
A berry grew not far from another berry,
One berry is Khvetis, sir,
And the other berry is Nastasyushka, dear.

Fyodor Tikhnavich is walking, cheerful.
He found the gold ring.
Gold with a precious stone.
Palagei Spanovich is walking, cheerless.
Palagei Spanovich lost the gold ring.
He lost the gold ring,
Gold with a precious stone.

Tally-ho, tally-ho
Tally-ho, dogs.
Tally-ho, hounds,
Tally-ho, cross-eyed (dogs)

A goose flew, she flew.
A grey goose flew, she flew.
She flapped her wings so much
That they made calluses.
She wobbled the posts
And woke up the boyars.

Father of the Groom:
Here's a wife for you chosen by God.
Druzhka:
Sow flax and hemp,
Ask her for shirts and pants.

Women:
We told you Nastyushka,
We told you, dear.

Mother of the Bride:
My darling son-in-law,
I give away my beloved daughter to you.

Druzhka, Mother of the Groom, and Svat:
Sow flax and hemp,
Ask her for shirts,
Give her drink, feed, and dress her,
And send her to work.
Cut wood, ask for cabbage soup,
Love her like a dear,
Shake her like a pear.

The boyars rose, and poured a cup.
They poured a cup and passed it around to

the guests,
To Marya they raised a toast:
"Drink, Maryushka, eat, Kharitonovna."
'I won't drink, I won't eat, I won't listen to the boyars."
"And if Simeon would ask?"
"I'd sing, I'd eat, I'd listen to the boyars."

Oh, you sparkling goose.
So where are you, sparkling goose.
Where did you go and what did you see?

I was on the blue sea, the lake,
On the very sea, the lake,
A white swan was bathing,
He paddled himself clean.

Have you been on the sea, white swan?
Did you see a lady swan, white swan?
How in the world could I not be on the sea?
How in the world could I a swan not see?
The swan has a lady under wing,
The swan has his darling under wing,
Khvetis has Nastasyushka to swing,
Khvetis has Timofeyevna under wing.

Druzhka:
So, Nastasyushka, what are you good for?

Bride:
I'm up to my neck in gold.
I have strings of pearls hanging to the ground.

Bolshoi Svat:
Ach, the sot, the drunkard is Nastya's father,
He swapped his child for a glass of wine,
For a glass of wine, for a cup of honey.

Druzhka:
Svashenki, hurry up!
Give us the bride, the groom is bored!

Pretty girls—cake masters, pot breakers;
Haughty wives, withered wives;
Little kids—jumping beans, carrot annihilators!
Sing a song!

Girls:
Khvetis will say: "I want to sleep."
And Nastasyushka will say: "And I with you."
Khvetis will say: "The bed is narrow."
And Nastasyushka will say: "It's wide enough for us."
Khvetis will say: "The blanket's cold."
And Nastasyushka will say: "It will be warm."

This is a song for Khvetis,
Who's a bright falcon
With a white swan,
Fair Nastasya Timofeyevna.
Are you listening, Khvetis, sir?
Are you listening, Pamfilich?

We're singing a song for you,
We're rendering you honor.

Svat with Poyezhannie:
Don't lie by the steep bank,
Don't sit, Savelushka, chatting.
Stock up for Khvetis's wedding.

Poyezhannie:
Ach, in the house there are drinks, and inside there's a wedding.
The boyars are at the table, they're drinking honey and wine,
And talking words:

"The provisions for my wedding are marvelous.
Nine vats of beer were brewed,
And the tenth vat, of green wine."

They lead Nastasyushka to a foreign land,
That girl will have to get used to living in a foreign land.
To be always a very obedient girl.

She who's obedient will fit in anywhere.
She'll bow low to old and young.
To the young girls, she'll bow even lower.

On the street, the street, on the wide street
The young fellow was walking, strolling,
Around the green garden, behind Nastya,
He bound a downy cap and violet ribbon to his head,
Khvetisushka looked and gazed
At his Nastyushka.
My Nastyushka has a quick walk,
A new fur coat, beaver trimming,

Druzhki:
Nastya with the black eyebrows!

Druzhki:
Now then, dear father, drink a shotglass,
Give presents to our kids!
Our kids need a lot of everything.
They want to have a full house,
They want to add on to the house, and put a steambath around the corner.
You'll come and take a steam bath.
And afterwards, youll boast about it:
Look at the way our kids live!

It's bitter, ach, bitter, ach, you can't drink this!

Well, come on, drink a shot glass,
And give presents to our kids.

This one, this one, she's full of spice,
And a rouble is still her price.
And if you blow her sides through,
They'd give even two.

Let it be like that,
Let it cost five roubles flat.
And then your honor it will be,
Even for a six rouble fee.

Druzhki and Women:
The River Volga is spilling over the ground,
At the gate, the son-in-law is hanging around,
Ach, my mother-in-law, my sweet mother-in-law.

Druzhka:
Or are you blind, druzhki?
You don't see that the girl nudged the boy's sides?
She called him to the cage.

Svat:
If you gave us the girl, now give the bed!

My bed, my bed,
On the bed is a feather bed,
On the feather bed is a headrest,
At the headrest theres a blanket,
Under the blanket theres a good fellow,
The good fellow Khvetisushka,
Khvetis Pamfilivich.

A sparrow pairs up with a lady sparrow,
Setting her on the bed.
Khvetisyushka kisses Nastasyushka.
He kisses her, caresses her, lays her on his hand,
On his hand, and presses her to his heart:
Oh you dear wife,
By day, the object of my gaze,
By night my amusement,
Well live life well,
So that people will envy us.

—translated from the Russian by Theodore Levin and Dmitri Pokrovsky

Reprinted courtesy of Elektra Nonesuch.

About the Participants

JOHN E. BOWLT is Professor of Slavic Language and Literature at the University of Southern California. His books include *Russian Art 1875-1975* (1976), *The Silver Age: Russian Art of the Early Twentieth Century* (1979), and *The Russian Avant-Garde: Theory and Criticsm 1902-34* (1988).

DENNIS RUSSELL DAVIES is Principal Conductor of the Brooklyn Philharmonic Orchestra. He also serves as Music Director of the American Composers Orchestra and General Music Director of the City of Bonn. This season, he conducts the New York Philharmonic and the Leipzig Gewandhaus Orchestra. He also appears regularly as a pianist.

LUKAS FOSS, Conductor Laureate of the Brooklyn Philharmonic Orchestra, has also served as Music Director of the Buffalo Philharmonic and of the Milwaukee Symphony. An intimate friend of Stravinsky's in California during the 1950's, he performed and recorded *Les noces* under Stravinsky's baton, and directed a 1965 Stravinsky festival for the New York Philharmonic.

JOSEPH HOROWITZ is Executive Director of the Brooklyn Philharmonic. His books are *Conversations with Arrau, Understanding Toscanini*, and *The Ivory Trade: Piano Competitions and the Business of Music*. His forthcoming study of Wagnerism in America, *Wagner Nights: An American History*, appears this October.

THEODORE LEVIN teaches in the Music Department at Dartmouth College. He is also a record producer specializing in music from the former Soviet Union. For many years, he conducted musical fieldwork in Central Eurasia, and is presently completing a book entitled *The 100,000 Fools of God: Musical Travels in Central Asia*.

DMITRI POKROVSKY studied conducting and balalaika at Moscow's Gnessin Institute. He formed the Pokrovsky Ensemble in 1973. Since then, the ensemble's repertoire has grown to encompass over 2,000 songs. It has toured the United States and Europe, has been featured in more then two dozen motion pictures, and appears regularly on Russian television. Its recordings include Stravinsky's *Les noces* on Elektra Nonesuch. Pokrovsky was awarded the State Prize of the USSR in 1989.

HENRY SCHUMAN is principal oboist of the Brooklyn Philharmonic Orchestra. Long an active chamber musician, he has played or conducted all the wind music of Stravinsky. He also performed and recorded *The Rite of Spring*, among other Stravinsky works, under Stravinsky's baton.

RICHARD TARUSKIN is Professor of Music at the University of California at Berkeley. His books include *Opera and Drama in Russia* (1981) and *Mussorgsky: Eight Essays and an Epilogue* (1993). His two-volume *Stravinsky and the Russian Traditions* will appear in 1995. He is also an experienced gambist and choral conductor.

ELIZABETH KRIDL VALKENIER is a Resident Scholar at Columbia University's W. Averell Harriman Institute for Advanced Study of the Soviet Union. She is the author of *Russian Realist Art, the State and Society* (1977), *The Soviet Union and the Third World: The Economic Bind* (1983), and *Ilya Repin and the World of Russian Art* (1990).

BROOKLYN PHILHARMONIC ORCHESTRA
DONORS
(List as of 4/12/94)

LEADERSHIP
($25,000 or more)
The Bernstein Education Through
 the Arts (BETA) Fund
Mary Flagler Cary
 Charitable Trust
Robert Sterling Clark Foundation
Rita & Stanley H. Kaplan
 Foundation
National Endowment
 for the Arts
National Endowment
 for the Humanities
New York City Department of
 Cultural Affairs
The New York
 Community Trust
New York State Council
 on the Arts
Edward John Noble Foundation
Philip Morris Companies Inc.
Republic National Bank/ Republic
 Bank for Savings
Robert C. Rosenberg
Starrett at Spring Creek,
 managed by
 Grenadier Realty Corp.
John Tamberlane
Trust for Mutual Understanding
Lila Wallace-Reader's Digest Fund

PACESETTERS
($10,000 or more)
Brooklyn Borough President
 Howard Golden
Brooklyn Union Gas
Kevin Burke
The Louis Calder Foundation
Con Edison
Delta Air Lines
Forest City Ratner Companies
The Fan Fox and Leslie R. Samuels
 Foundation, Inc.
Stanley H. Kaplan Educational
 Center
Craig G. Matthews
Meet The Composer
Music Performance Trust Funds
National Westminster
 Bank USA
Julie & Bruce Ratner
The Scherman Foundation, Inc.
Selectimpex
 Bank of Moscow
Emma A. Sheafer
 Charitable Trust
Paul Travis
Michael Tuch Foundation

PATRONS
($5,000 or more)
A&S
The Louis Armstrong Educational
 Foundation, Inc.
Bank Leumi
Chemical Bank

Eleanor Naylor Dana Charitable
 Trust
Aaron Diamond Foundation
The Equitable Foundation
Susan Fletcher
The Gallery at MetroTech Center
Amerada Hess Corporation
Independence Savings Bank
Richard Kane
The J.M. Kaplan Fund
J.P. Morgan Charitable Trust
New York City.
 Yours to Discover
 Tourism Grant Program
New York Newsday
Pfizer Inc.
The Billy Rose Foundation
Helena Rubinstein Foundation
Janet Scherer
Starr Foundation

GRANTORS
($2,500 or more)
Jim Anderson &
 Phoebe Ferguson
The Barker Welfare Foundation
Botwinick-Wolfensohn Foundation
Jane Brody & Richard Engquist
The Chase Manhattan Bank, NA
The Dime Savings Bank
 of New York
European American Bank
The Fund for the
 Borough of Brooklyn
Joyce Mertz-Gilmore Foundation
Goldie-Anna Charitable Trust
The Heckscher Foundation
 for Children
Jerry Jacobs
Harvey & Phyllis Lichtenstein
Merrill Lynch
Harry A. Olson, Jr.
John M. Powers, Jr.
Joseph R. Small
Laura Walker & Bert Wells

CHAMPIONS
($1,500 or more)
Mrs. F. Henry Berlin
Ann & Gordon Getty Foundation
Ronald Greene
Merrill G. & Emita E. Hastings
 Foundation
The Victor Herbert Foundation
IBM Corporation
Nicholas M. Infantino
Mr. & Mrs. Harvey Kaylie

DONORS
($1,000 or more)
Bangser Klein Rocca & Blum
Cowles Charitable Trust
Gerard Conn & Carol Yorke
Gary P. Gailes
Goldman Sachs
Mr. & Mrs. Fred Haber

Mr. & Mrs. Richard W. Hulbert
Mr. & Mrs. Joseph F. Kelly
I. Stanley Kriegel
Mr. Jonathan Leader
In Memory of
 Bernard L. Rosenberg
Arnold L. Sabin
Mr. & Mrs. William Weinpahl

BENEFACTORS
($500 or more)
A A Air Filters
Alan & Leslie Beller
Ernie & Rita Bogen
Constans Culver Foundation
Domino Sugar Corporation
Greenpoint Savings Bank
The Rev. Louis Hallgring
Mrs. Walter Hinrichsen
John Barch Construction
Mrs. August Ludtmann
Peerless Importers
Mr. & Mrs. Frederick P. Rose
Salomon Brothers Inc.
Securities Industry Automation
 Corporation (SIAC)
Clifford Siegel
Stadtmauer, Bailkin, Levine & Masyr
Dr. Arthur J. Vidich

SUSTAINERS
($250 or more)
Anbro Supply Co., Inc.
Seymour & Lillian Besunder
John D. Brown
Leo Castelli
Central Elevator
Dr. and Mrs. Wen Jer Chen
Mr. James Collins
Mr. & Mrs. George Costa
Denver Investment Advisors
Mr. Stan Eckstut
Feld Kaminetzky & Cohen, P.C.
Mr. & Mrs. Darko V. Frank
Mendel Gurfein
Mr. & Mrs. Gerard Hekker
F.J. Kazeroid Realty Group
Mr. & Mrs. Jessie Kelly
Alice Kupper
Stephen Lefkowitz
Marjorie Martin
Daniel McCrary
Dr. Tatsuji Namba
James B. Patrick
Mr. & Mrs. Peter Pfau
Mr. Rubin Raskin
Ms. Dawn B. Roadman
Ms. Elaine F. Rubenstein
Dr. & Mrs. Martin J. Salwen
Mr. & Mrs. Henry Schlittner
Mrs. George P. Schmidt
Martin & Edith Segal
Paul D. Selver
Mr. & Mrs. Robert Shapiro
Mr. & Mrs. Rolland G. Smith
Dr. Susan Stewart

Thomas W. Streeter
Drs. B. & E. Wainfeld
Mr. & Mrs. Joel Wechsler
Mr. & Mrs. Herbert Weller
Richard Wood
Zeitz Foundation

CONTRIBUTORS
($150 or more)
C. Murray Adams
Igou & Nedda Allbray
Sarah Jean Avery
Mr. Denis Azaro
Ernest R. Bitzer
Jean-Marie Blondeau
Janice B. Brown
John D. Brown
Castle Oil Corporation
Dr. & Mrs. Clifford Cohen
Richard Corry
Richard Crisona
Kevin F. Cronebach
Dennis & Brenda Dugan
Dwight & Ann Ellis
Mrs. Vincent Finamore
Mrs. Wanatha Garner
Dr. Abraham &
 Mrs. Anita Gilner
Mr. David Grunblatt
Mr. John D. Haney
Ms. Consuelo Hudgins
Mr. & Mrs. Michael Janove
Mr. Robert B. Jones
Jessie & Dennis Kelly
Frank Robert Kraft
Richard M. Lagani
Sam & Stephanie Lebowitz
Charlton M. Lewis III
Ms. Nancy Lynch
Mr. Sam Marcus
Clark Marlor
Ms. Lorraine E. Mones
David & Sheila Newman
Robert C. Newman
John E. O'Connor
Mr. & Mrs. Carl A. Palumbo
Mr. Ronald F. Reis
Ronnie Ringel
Mr. Benjamin Rottenstein
Samuel Schwartz
Harvey Seiderbaum
Hildy Simmons &
 David Sprafkin
Nicholas Stathis
Warren A. Sweeney
Darius Toraby, R.A.
Mr. Staffan Wahlander
Ms. Claire Weidman
Susan Whiting &
 Bruce Van Dusen
Dr. & Mrs. Edward Wolf

BPO also wishes to thank donors making gifts of less than $150, and especially the ADOPT-A-TEEN
sponsors of the In-School Performance and Instruction Program.
If you would like information on becoming a contributor to BPO, please contact the Development Office at 718-636-4137.

THE BROOKLYN PHILHARMONIC ORCHESTRA
salutes the sponsors of its 1993/94 SOUNDWAVE season and donors to
The Russian Stravinsky

Leadership support for THE RUSSIAN STRAVINSKY has been provided by
The Division of Public Programs, Public Humanities Projects
of the National Endowment for the Humanities,
Selectimpex Bank of Moscow, Russia
and the
Trust for Mutual Understanding.
The 1993/94 SOUNDWAVE Season is sponsored by Philip Morris Companies Inc.

BPO's Russian Stravinsky Gala, celebrating the Orchestra's 40th Anniversary, has been made
possible by Republic National Bank of New York and Republic Bank for Savings.

BPO is proud to be the recipient of a National Endowment for the Arts Challenge III Grant.

Delta Air Lines is the official airline of the Brooklyn Philharmonic Orchestra.

BPO's Education Program is supported by a generous grant from
Starrett at Spring Creek, managed by Grenadier Realty Corp.

Additional major support has been provided by:
Mary Flagler Cary Charitable Trust
New York City Department of Cultural Affairs
Edward John Noble Foundation
Robert C. Rosenberg
Rita J. & Stanley H. Kaplan Foundation
Stanley H. Kaplan Educational Center
New York State Council on the Arts
Brooklyn Union Gas
The Fan Fox & Leslie R. Samuels Foundation, Inc.
Brooklyn Borough President Howard Golden

BPO's Audience Development initiatives have been supported by
The Robert Sterling Clark Foundation and The New York Community Trust.

The SOUNDWAVE Bus to Opera House events is sponsored by
Independence Savings Bank.

BPO'S 40TH ANNIVERSARY RUSSIAN STRAVINSKY GALA

Gala Chair
John Tamberlane
President, Republic Bank for Savings

Honorary Gala Chair
Cynthia Gregory

Gala Committee
Bettina Bancroft
Honorable Herb Berman

Mrs. F. Henry Berlin
Norman J. Buchan
Honorable Schuyler G. Chapin
Honorable Howard Golden
Fredric J. Hugue
Richard Kane
Stanley H. Kaplan
I. Stanley Kriegel
Harvey & Phyllis Lichtenstein
Shahara Ahmad-Llewellyn & J. Bruce Llewellyn

Craig G. Matthews
Senator Velmanette Montgomery
John M. Powers, Jr.
Julie & Bruce Ratner
Robert C. Rosenberg & Fran Kaufman
Janet Scherer
Honorable Edolphus Towns
Paul Travis
Honorable Peter F. Vallone
Evelyn "Tessie" Williams

The Brooklyn Philharmonic Orchestra

The Brooklyn Philharmonic Orchestra, now celebrating its 40th Anniversary and in its third season under Principal Conductor Dennis Russell Davies, is the Resident Orchestra of the Brooklyn Academy of Music. Its Conductor Laureate, Lukas Foss, served as Music Director from 1971 to 1990.

The Orchestra remains committed to expanding the symphonic repertoire and to the parallel development of innovative educational and community programming. Among BPO's honors are fourteen American Symphony Orchestra League/ASCAP creative programming awards, and a National Endowment for the Arts Challenge III Award for new artistic initiatives (1991 to June 1994).

This season, the BPO's main subscription series - entitled SOUNDWAVE - consists of *The Russian Stravinsky* and four other thematically integrated, interdisciplinary festivals incorporating discussions and symposia as well as film, dance, theater, and the visual arts. These SOUNDWAVE programs include American or New York premieres of works by Jiri Anton Benda, Henryk Gorecki, Giya Kancheli, Arvo Pärt, and Duke Ellington.

The Orchestra's additional educational and community programs reach over 50,000 individuals annually. Its Free Schooltime Concerts, under conductor David Amram, enable schoolchildren to hear, often for the first time, both folk and symphonic music from around the world. The In-School Performance and Instruction Program provides students with one-on-one rehearsal and performance experiences with professional musicians. The Orchestra's Free Summer Parks and Community Concerts take place in neighborhoods throughout greater New York.

BPO performances are frequently heard on national radio broadcasts. Its most recent recordings, under Dennis Russell Davies, include works by Philip Glass, Peggy Glanville-Hicks, Lou Harrison, and Terry Riley.

DMITRI POKROVSKY ENSEMBLE
Dmitri Pokrovsky: Artistic Director
Abigail Adams: Manager

Tamara Smyslova	Svetlana Dorokhova	Igor Chaplynsky	Dmitri Fokin	Michael Korzin
Elena Sergeyeva	Marina Cherkashina	Alevtina Popova	Alexander Prianikov	Alexander Danilov
Olga Uketcheva	Irene Ivashkina	Eygenny Vedernikov	Dmitri Grishin	Eygenny Tarasov
Maria Nefiodova	Olga Tomashenko	Sergei Zhirkov	Alexander Gordyenko	Oleg Kazancheyev
Valentia Kozlova				

BROOKLYN PHILHARMONIC ORCHESTRA
MAY 6, 7, 8
(all lists as of 4/12/94)

Violin I
Benjamin Hudson, Concertmaster
Yuval Waldman
Carlos Villa
Rebekah Johnson
Ann Labin
Katsuko Esaki
Thomas Suarez
Gayle Dixon
Michael Levin
Nam Sook Lee
Liang Chai
Qing Guo
Ellen Jewett
Katherine Hannauer
Christine Sunnerstam
Alexander Yudkovsky

Violin II
Darryl Kubian, Principal
Dale Stuckenbruck
Eugenie Seid Kroop
Fritz Krakowski
Sebu Sirinian
Rena Isbin
Shin Won Kim
Naomi Katz
Lisa Tipton
Gabriel Schaff
Elmira Belkin
Elizabeth Miller
Louellen Abdoo
Robert Zubrycki

Viola
Sarah Adams, Principal
Ron Carbone
Nancy Usher
Monica Gerard

Leslie Tomkins
Juliette Haffner
Karen Ritscher
Maxine Roach
Richard Brice
Christine Ims

Cello
Chris Finkel, Principal
David Calhoun
Lanny Paykin
Michael Rudiakov
Frank Murphy
Peter Rosenfeld
Sally Cline
Sarah Fiene
Stan Orlovsky

Bass
Joe Bongiorno, Principal
Marji Danilow
Lou Bruno
Janet Conway Barbour
Jules Hirsh
Richard Sosinsky
Deb Spohnheimer

Flute
Katherine Fink, Principal
David Wechsler
Helen Campo
Wendy Stern
Susan Rotholz

Oboe
Henry Schuman, Principal
Richard D'Allessio
Robert Walters
Mary Watt

Clarinet
Steve Hartman, Principal
Laura Flax
Dennis Smylie
Larry Guy
Mitchel Weiss

Bassoon
Harry Searing, Principal
Jeffrey Marchand
Gilbert Dejean
Tom Sefcovic
Don McGeen

French Horn
Paul Ingraham, Principal
Scott Temple
Richard Hagen
John Clark
Dan Culpepper
Kait Mahony
Glen Estrin
Fred Griffen

Trumpet
Wilmer Wise, Principal
James Stubbs, Co-Principal
Phillip Ruecktenwald
Neil Balm
Cari Sakovsky
Alex Holton

Trombone
Jonathan Taylor, Principal
Hugh Eddy
Lawrence Benz
Tom Olcott

Tuba
Andrew Seligson,
Principal
Steve Johns

Timpani
Richard Fitz, Principal

Percussion
James Preiss, Principal
David Frost
William Trigg
Louis Oddo
Gordon Gottlieb
Charles Descarfino

Harp
Karen Lindquist
Tory Drake

Keyboard
Ken Bowen
William Grossman

Cimbalom
Ron Snider

* * *

Personnel for
Renard (May 8)

Violin I
Benjamin Hudson

Violin II
Darryl Kubian

Viola
Sarah Adams

Cello
Chris Finkel

Bass
Joe Bongiorno

Flute
Katherine Fink

Oboe
Henry Schuman

Clarinet
Steve Hartman

French Horn
Paul Ingraham
Scott Temple

Trumpet
Wilmer Wise

Timpani
Richard Fitz

Percussion
James Preiss
David Frost

Cimbalom
Ron Snider

BROOKLYN PHILHARMONIC ORCHESTRA BOARD AND STAFF

Richard Taruskin and John E. Bowlt graciously provided assistance in gathering and reproducing illustrations and photographs for this publication, as did Sam Rosenthal, Rose Vekony, and Doris Kretschmer of the University of California Press.

Illustrations on pages 54 and 55: from the collection of Mr. & Mrs. Nikita D. Lobanov-Rostovsky, London.

Cover design based on "Xylographies," an engraving by Wassily Kandinsky, (1909); State Gallery in Lenbachhaus, Munich.

Photographs on pages 5, 9, 13, 17, 18, 37, and 42 courtesy of Special Collections, Music Division of the New York Public Library at Lincoln Center.